D0031561

Molly

The True Story of the Dog Who Rescues Lost Cats

Molly

The True Story of the Dog Who Rescues Lost Cats

COLIN BUTCHER

Feiwel and Friends
New York

A FEIWEL AND FRIENDS BOOK
An imprint of Macmillan Publishing Group, LLC
120 Broadway, New York, NY 10271
mackids.com

Our books may be purchased in bulk for promotional, educational, or business
use. Please contact your local bookseller or the Macmillan Corporate and
Premium Sales Department at (800) 221-7945 ext. 5442 or by email at
MacmillanSpecialMarkets@macmillan.com.

Library of Congress Cataloging-in-Publication Data is available.

First US Edition, 2019
First Feiwel & Friends Edition, 2022
Book design by Trisha Previte
All photographs courtesy of the author
Feiwel and Friends logo designed by Filomena Tuosto

Printed in the United States of America by
LSC Communications, Harrisonburg, Virginia.

ISBN 978-1-250-20705-0 (hardcover)

10   9   8   7   6   5   4   3   2   1

Originally published as *Molly and Me* in the UK by Michael Joseph, Penguin
Random House UK

For David

They are called sleuth-hounds by the people. These dogs have such a marvelous cleverness that they seek for thieves, and follow them only by the scent of the goods that are taken away.

—*The History and Croniklis of Scotland* (1536) by John Bellenden (Scots translation of Hector Boece's *Historia Gentis Scotorum*)

Molly

The True Story of the Dog Who Rescues Lost Cats

1

MOLLY'S FIRST TEST

At 9 a.m. on Friday, 3 February 2017, just as my assistant, Sam, had settled at her desk, the telephone rang. I was outside in the early-morning sun, preparing to exercise Molly.

My cocker spaniel had woken up in a particularly frisky mood—so much so that she'd knocked over my girlfriend Sarah's favorite vase in the hallway. Molly needed to run off some energy.

"UK Pet Detectives," answered Sam. "Can we help?"

"I really hope so," replied a glum male voice. "Our cat, Rusty, has gone missing. We've looked everywhere, but there's no sign of her. We've hit a brick wall, really, so we thought we'd give you guys a call."

The man went on to explain that his name was Tim, and he and his girlfriend, Jasmine, lived in a first-floor apartment in a building on a quiet cul-de-sac. They were

Me and Sam at Pet Detective HQ

both cat-lovers, and had adopted Rusty, a black-white-and-copper rescue with almond-shaped eyes and a long, fluffy tail. They often let the cat outdoors, where she'd hang around the street, lazing on driveways and sitting on doorsteps, never straying too far or staying out late.

The previous Friday, however, Rusty had failed to turn up for her weekly treat of steamed fish, and her owners were surprised and concerned.

"It's just so out of character," Tim told Sam. "We've spent the whole weekend searching in streets and gardens—we've even printed out leaflets and posters—but she's nowhere to be found. We're at a total loss."

"I'm so sorry to hear that," said Sam. "Leave it to me. I'll have a word with my boss and I'll get back to you."

She promptly bounded over to the large window and yanked it up.

"*COLIN!*" she yelled, stopping Molly and me dead in our tracks. "Make sure you pop in after your training session. Think I might have found Molly's first proper job . . ."

Half an hour later I was discussing Rusty's disappearance with Sam while a worn-out Molly enjoyed a snooze. I felt my pulse quicken as Sam outlined the missing pet's circumstances. If our inaugural cat-seeking assignment was to be a success, the search conditions had to be as favorable as possible. This one seemed to check all the boxes.

Rusty came from a single-cat household, thus enabling me to obtain a decent hair sample and giving Molly the best chance of isolating the scent and matching it to the lost cat. Secondly, Rusty had been missing for a week, which increased the likelihood of finding her alive. Also working in our favor was the fact that the weather was calm and settled, unseasonably so, in fact, for early February. Strong winds or any form of precipitation (rain, snow or mist, for example) would dilute the cat scent and interfere with my dog's ultra-sensitive nose.

Luckily, I was well versed in all things meteorological and geographical. Prior to my long career in the police force I'd spent over a decade in the Royal Navy, becoming something of an expert on air masses, frontal systems and cartography. Little did I know then how useful this knowledge would become in the world of pet detection.

In December 2016 Molly had completed intensive scent-recognition training, and since then she and I had staged countless practice scenarios at my Bramble Hill Farm HQ, honing our skills in preparation for our first real-life search for a missing cat. I had been confident that Molly and I had attained the required level of competence, but it was only when I'd sent some video footage of our training to the experts at the Medical Detection Dogs charity that we'd finally been given the green light.

"From what we've seen, we think you're both ready for your first proper search," they'd said, causing a tingle to shoot up my spine. "Your interaction and teamwork are excellent and, as far as we're concerned, you're good to go."

Now I faced the prospect of solving a live search with Molly by my side. I felt a mixture of exhilaration and nervousness. I had spent so much time and energy developing my innovative cat-detection-dog idea—it had been five years in the making. Having found my perfect sidekick, I was desperate to prove that all our hard work had been worth it.

"This could be it," I said to Sam. "This could be Molly's first test."

"Oh my goodness, how exciting!" She grinned.

That evening I spent an hour or so on the phone with Tim, obtaining as much background information as possible. I asked him whether there'd been any triggers that might have caused Rusty to flee, but Tim was adamant that, as far as he was concerned, nothing had changed.

"The elderly lady who lives in the opposite flat died last week, which was quite upsetting," he said, "but other than that, things have been pretty humdrum around here."

As for sightings, they'd drawn a blank in their own neighborhood. But that morning they had received calls from two separate witnesses in a village a few miles away who claimed to have seen a cat answering Rusty's description in their respective gardens.

"I doubt it's our cat, because she's never, ever roamed that far," admitted Tim, "but we'd still like you to investigate, if you don't mind."

"I'm more than happy to help," I replied, before casually mentioning that I'd be accompanied by a canine colleague.

"My cocker spaniel, Molly, will be coming, too," I said. "She's got a decent sense of smell and she doesn't yap at cats so she might be quite useful. Hope that's okay with you."

I was purposely downplaying things, so as not to put any pressure upon Molly, or myself.

"No problem," said Tim. "Anything that might help us find Rusty is fine with me."

I spent the rest of the night poring over digital maps, plans and photos of the St. Albans area where Tim and Jasmine lived while Sarah slept beside me. It was important that I learned as much as possible about the neighborhood so as to give Molly and me the best chance of locating Rusty. When I felt myself beginning to nod off, I shut down my laptop and went to check on Molly, as I did every night. She sensed me peering through the gap in the door, raised her head and drowsily opened one eye.

Molly's first meeting at Medical Detection Dogs (MDD)

"We've got a big day ahead, young lady," I whispered, "so I'll see you bright and early in the morning."

Yeah, I know, Dad, Molly seemed to say, *so how's about letting me get some sleep?*

She held my gaze for a couple of seconds before curling up tight and going back to sleep.

We left the house at 5 a.m. The weather was cool and cloudy with a slight underlying breeze: the perfect conditions for our big search, I hoped. Sarah had seen us off, fully aware of the magnitude of the next few hours. She had watched me build up to this moment for a long time and knew exactly how much it meant to me. "Hope it all goes well, darling." She'd smiled, and I almost did a double-take when she gently, yet gingerly, patted Molly's glossy black head before wishing her good luck. Sarah was no dog-lover and her rare display of affection for Molly meant a lot.

Molly literally lapped it up, giving Sarah's palm a big, sloppy lick in return for her kind words. I smiled, imagining Sarah darting straight to the hand sanitizer as soon as she returned indoors.

It was a two-hour drive from West Sussex to Tim and Jasmine's apartment in Hertfordshire. They greeted us outside their modern four-story building. I guessed they were in their mid-twenties, and both wore a kind of glazed expression that I recognized only too well. Like many of my clients before them, their precious pet had gone missing, and they were sick to their stomachs with worry.

My eye was drawn to a huge poster in their front window. PLEASE HELP, I'M LOST, it declared. CAN YOU HELP ME FIND MY HOME?

Staring out from behind the printed text was a beautiful photograph of Rusty. She was a pretty cat with a friendly face. She had a white chest and legs, and two black splotches above her eyes, which made her look like a feline caped crusader.

"I wish all my clients could produce something so professional-looking," I said.

"Being a graphic designer comes in handy sometimes . . . ," replied Tim with a wan smile.

". . . and our Rusty is a dream to photograph," added Jasmine.

I followed the couple indoors, leaving Molly safe and secure in the car (and, as always, in my line of vision) with her favorite toys for company. I knew that she'd experience serious sensory overload if she entered an unfamiliar flat, and I needed her to remain as calm as possible. It was crucial that she would be able to focus solely on Rusty's scent, if I was lucky enough to obtain a decent sample.

The three of us discussed a plan of action. Jasmine

had to work that morning, so Tim would accompany Molly and me on the search. Our first stop would be the nearby village where the two cat sightings had occurred, but before we set off I posed a question.

"I know this may sound a little odd, Tim, but would you mind if I took a sample of Rusty's cat hair? Molly's a trained sniffer dog and—you never know—she might detect some scent."

I wanted to keep things nicely understated. I needed to manage Tim's expectations so that he didn't start believing that the deployment of a search dog would guarantee Rusty's recovery.

"Yeah, sure, help yourself," he replied. "She molts a lot. Her cat bed's full of it."

Out came my sterilized jam jar, and in went a wad of whitish hair; more than enough for Molly to get her amazing nose into.

Molly and I had often practiced the transition from pet mode to work mode at Bramble Hill Farm, and donning our respective "uniforms" had always been a vital part of this routine. So I strapped on Molly's special harness once I got her out of the car and zipped up my United Kingdom Pet Detective fleece. I was buzzing with excitement but did my utmost to adopt a professional demeanor.

As Tim and I surveyed our surroundings a brisk wind began to whip up, with enough vigor to ruffle our hair. *This wasn't forecast*, I thought. I looked to the horizon and saw the telltale signs of a warm front heading our way. I knew this would bring steady winds for the rest of the day, followed by rain. I figured that we had about six hours before the first drops reached us.

"We really need to get started, Tim," I said, looking at my watch.

"Okay," he said. "Let's go for it."

The two gardens that Rusty had reportedly been sighted in were on opposite sides of the road and, fortunately, both owners allowed us access. With a deep breath and my heart racing, I introduced Rusty's cat-hair sample to Molly for the first time. I unscrewed the jam jar and gave my command of *Toma*, which means "take" in Spanish. The expert trainers at MDD forensic accountants had selected the command since Molly would never hear the word spoken around my house or within any other context.

I offered the jar up to Molly's snout.

She inhaled the scent and waited for my next command.

"Seek, seek," I said. As soon as I did, she belted off into the first garden, her tail wagging furiously.

"Oh, wow . . . ," said Tim, slowly realizing that Molly was not your average dog. "Has she . . . has she been trained to do this?"

"She has." I smiled. "But, Tim, you need to know

that this is her first live search and it would be unfair to you—and Molly—if I was to promise anything. But she'll do her very best to find Rusty, I can assure you of that."

Molly searched everywhere for the cat's scent—beneath a holly bush, inside the greenhouse, behind the compost pile—but to no avail. All the while, she increased her eye contact with me, which meant that she had finished sweeping the area.

There's no cat here, Dad . . . let's go . . . was how I read her body language.

It was a similar story in the second garden. Molly failed to locate any scent trails and I was pretty sure that Rusty had never ventured there. However, as I called her with a command of "Molly, come," I noticed a black-gray-and-tan cat tiptoeing across the lawn. I squinted as it came closer.

Oh my goodness, I thought. *Is that Rusty walking toward me? Is Molly having an "off" day?*

"THAT'S HER!" squawked the homeowner from her kitchen window. "That's the cat I saw!"

Tim nearly jumped out of his skin, but his reaction when he caught sight of the animal was telling. Molly had remained unmoved, too, which should have told me all I needed to know.

"That's not her," said Tim, shaking his head sadly. "Same coloring, but different markings. Rusty's got this really weird half-pink, half-black nose. I'd recognize her anywhere."

Crestfallen after this case of mistaken identity, we went for coffee and got Molly some water, which she slurped noisily from a large bowl. She needed plenty of breaks and drinks when she was on a search, and I made sure that she was never overworked. I didn't want her to suffer from scenting fatigue (also known as "nose blindness"), which would cause her to lose the ability to isolate Rusty's odor.

To get more clues about Rusty's disappearance, I quizzed Tim about his neighborhood. The subject of the deceased old lady in the apartment building cropped up again so I pressed for more information. According to Tim, she'd been taken away in an ambulance. This nugget of information got me wondering.

"Do you happen to remember which day your neighbor passed away?" I said.

"Erm, let me think," he replied, counting back with his fingers. "Friday. Yeah, it must have been last Friday."

"The same day that Rusty went missing?"

Tim paused for a moment, furrowing his brow.

"Yes . . . I suppose it would have been. I know what you're thinking, Colin, but Rusty had a fear of cars. She associated them with being taken to the vet's."

"Private ambulances tend not to be cars, though,"

I explained. In fact, most of them were large, roomy minibuses with blacked-out windows and easy-access ramps. My detective instincts kicked in. "Can you give me a couple of minutes? I need to make a few phone calls."

I rang the local general practitioner, who informed me that the lady's body had been transported by a private ambulance to the funeral directors' chapel in Stonebridge—about a mile away from Tim's home. The vehicle—a large, dark blue minibus—had been parked outside their offices for the rest of the day. Slowly but surely, the jigsaw pieces were beginning to come together.

I headed out to the parking lot (with a fully refreshed Molly in tow) and found Tim.

"Right," I said briskly. "I'm starting to think this may be a case of accidental transportation."

I told him that there was a very real possibility that Rusty had snuck into the ambulance outside the apartment building and been driven off by accident. The timeline of events definitely made sense, and it would explain the sudden nature of her disappearance.

"Next stop, Stonebridge," I said.

While the funeral directors' receptionist confirmed the ambulance's route, she'd received no reports of a cat being found inside. She did admit, however, that the vehicle's rear doors would have been opened and closed on numerous occasions.

"Sorry I can't be more helpful," she said, "but you might want to speak to the ladies at the post office next door. If there's any news or gossip flying around, they'll know about it."

She wasn't wrong. The employees behind the counter at the post office took a real shine to Molly and agreed to display one of Tim's posters on the noticeboard. As I was hanging it, an elderly gentleman walked in, took one look at Rusty's photo and gasped.

"That cat was on our fence this morning, I'm sure of it," he declared. "Beautiful creature, lovely bushy tail. Remember my wife saying that she'd never seen it before. Oh, and it had this really strange-looking nose . . ."

Tim grabbed my arm in excitement.

"Can you possibly take us to your garden now?" I asked.

Ten minutes later I was crouching outside old Mr. Renshaw's red-brick home, going through the scent-sniffing routine with Molly for the second time that day. With Rusty's odor coursing through her nostrils, she sprinted into the back garden and within seconds gave her trademark success signal.

Wham-*bam*, Molly was "down" in the center of the

lawn! She was using the rapid response that had been drilled into her during training. It was a move that let her alert her handler without alarming any cats. She was lying flat, still and silent, with her front paws outstretched, her back legs tucked under her body, her head upright and her eyes locked. Her body quivered with excitement at the thrill of the "victory" and the expectation of a reward for her achievement.

My heart began to pound like a drum. We had practiced this drill so often at Bramble Hill Farm, but this was the first time that I'd seen her do it for a real-life client.

"What does that mean?" whispered Tim as he watched Molly trembling before us.

"She's signaling that she's detected a high concentration of Rusty's scent," I replied, "so you can be pretty certain that your cat has been here fairly recently. We just need to work out where she is now."

While a pepped-up Tim texted Jasmine, I rewarded Molly for doing her job. She'd made a scent match, despite the cat herself not being present. Molly's favorite black-pudding treats were munched in a millisecond.

I wanted to figure out why Molly had "downed" in the dead center of the garden and why Rusty's scent had accumulated at that specific point. I stood at the precise spot where Molly had lain and turned to face the wind. The breeze was coming directly across the fence, which would have forced the air upward, causing it to roll across the lawn like a wave and washing the scent to the exact place where Molly had indicated.

What a good girl, Molly, I thought. *She's absolutely spot-on.*

With Rusty very likely to be in the immediate area, it was now vital that I invested all my faith in Molly. I employed a strategic and methodical approach. First and foremost, we had to narrow down the search area. There were about thirty houses on Mr. Renshaw's side of the road, and beyond those houses' long, sixty-foot gardens lay a huge stretch of farmland. We needed to pinpoint the properties that seemed most promising. We'd already lost half the day looking in the wrong village, so I decided to run Molly along a gravel footpath that divided the residents' gardens from the farmers' fields. As we passed a couple of adjoining houses, I noticed her become very focused and spin a number of 180-degree turns. This was often a sure sign that she'd detected something significant.

"Tim, could you do me a favor and knock on the owners' front doors?" I asked. "Molly's desperate to get in and we'll need their say-so."

The first house—number 36—was occupied by two elderly sisters who, despite being somewhat bewildered, were more than happy for us to search their grounds.

Molly shot through the back gate like an arrow and darted into one of the most pristine gardens I'd ever seen.

My keyed-up dog zigzagged around ornamental birdbaths and Japanese plant pots, churning up the manicured lawn as she went. Her swishing tail sliced the heads off paper-thin flowers.

"I'm really sorry about this," I told the sisters. "I can put her on a lead, if you prefer."

"Absolutely not!" one replied. "This is fascinating . . ."

Then Molly slammed on her brakes and executed another 180-degree turn, before veering off toward their freshly painted garden fence and scraping her sharp claws down the dark green panels. Her intensity levels were increasing. I just needed to know why.

I wanna go next door, I wanna go next door, she seemed to be saying, her eyes searching mine for some guidance. *Let. Me. Go. Next. Door.*

"Bear with me, Molly," I whispered.

I peered over the fence. A middle-aged woman and a teenage boy were standing on their patio, clearly wondering about all the noise and commotion coming from their neighbors' house. Their garden wasn't as ornate as the sisters' yard, I noted.

"Can we come over, please?" I yelled, giving them a quick explanation, then dashing to their front gate with Molly and Tim in tow. Meanwhile, a small group of people, including one of the post-office employees, had congregated on the pavement outside; news of the Missing Cat and the Detection Dog had clearly traveled.

I gave Molly the signal to proceed, and she charged across number 38's lawn. She didn't even break stride when she gobbled up some bacon rind that had been left out for the birds. She then sprang onto the deck, whirled around, locked her eyes with mine, and gave me the most emphatic "down" I'd ever seen her give.

"Oh my god, she's doing that trembly thing again," whispered Tim, his voice shaking. "Has she found her?"

"One moment . . . ," I said, creeping stealthily toward an outbuilding in the garden and peering through its glass door, which was slightly ajar.

Sitting in a dark corner, atop a blue cushion, was a cat. A white-black-and-copper cat. An almond-eyed, bushy-tailed cat. A pink-and-black-nosed cat.

"RUSTY!" cried Tim, unable to control his emotions. "My cat!!! Molly's found my cat!!!"

"A cat? No *waaaay* . . . ," drawled the teenage son.

"That's what happens when your dad doesn't lock the door properly," tutted his mother. "Poor little thing."

Within seconds, perhaps spooked by her owner's

hooting and hollering, Rusty shot out of the building and up the driveway, scampering through a succession of front gardens.

Tim sprinted after her, hurdling the hedges like an Olympic runner. He eventually caught up with her and scooped her up from beneath a hazel bush. I put Molly on a lead and hurried after him. When we reached them, Tim was cradling his cat in his arms, tears of joy streaming down his cheeks.

"I don't know what to say," he sobbed. "I just can't believe you've found her. Thank you, Colin. Thank you, Molly. Thank you *so, so* much."

A spontaneous ripple of applause rang out from the assembled neighbors.

"Most exciting thing that's happened in the village for years," said one, laughing.

The sisters at number 36 kindly allowed Tim to take Rusty indoors for a while, where she *glugged* a bowlful of water and devoured a pouch of cat food that had been donated by another neighbor. As he sat at the kitchen table, Tim relayed the happy news to Jasmine by phone.

Poor Rusty had clearly roamed around the village after her ambulance ride in search of shelter, warmth, food and water—every cat's basic needs. She must have found the outbuilding at number 38 and settled in there.

It had been a very good decision on her part. The building had acted as a sanctuary, offering her shelter, and the protein-rich bacon rind that had been left for the birds would have provided vital sustenance. Rusty even had access to water from the birdbaths in the garden next door.

"She's a smart little cookie, according to Colin," Tim explained to Jasmine, half laughing, half crying.

Back outside, I let everything sink in and my eyes began to mist over. Four years previously I'd first set out to find and train a cat-detection dog, and had figured it would take me about six months. In the end, I'd devoted hundreds of hours to researching the idea and had traveled thousands of miles to meet the country's

Molly and Me—the perfect pet-detective duo

top experts. I'd also overcome a great deal of resistance and hostility. So many people had told me that it couldn't be done.

But today I had seen that it could be done. Thanks to Molly, I finally had proof that my idea could work. She and I had solved the case and reunited a pet with its owner.

I knelt down and gently brushed my hand against the side of Molly's face. It was one of her favorite places to be scratched.

"Can you believe it, Molly?" I smiled as she gently nibbled the inside of my palm. "We've gone and found our first missing cat!"

Stealing a quick look over my shoulder to make sure we were alone, I jumped into the air and yelled *YES!* as loudly as I could. Molly was taken by surprise at first, but then she leaped up high and started barking her very own *YES!* We were so caught up in our celebration that we were totally oblivious that a heavy rain had begun to fall.

SCENTING SUCCESS

My pet-detecting skills can be traced all the way back to the summer of 1989, when I first joined the Surrey Police Department. In my early days as an officer I'd become accustomed to dealing with stressful situations and unsavory characters. Being a rookie, however, meant that I was also assigned to some of the more mundane incidents, including missing-pet reports.

One autumn morning early in my career I was told to check on an elderly woman who had reported her cat missing, and I found myself questioning whether this case was a priority.

"Isn't this a bit, er, trivial?" I asked.

"On the contrary," replied my superior. "It's important that we're visible in the community, whether it's a lost cat or a runaway dog."

I didn't realize it at the time, but dealing with these seemingly minor issues would help me enormously later on. Getting to know the neighborhood—and securing the confidence of residents—was often vital when investigating a serious crime.

Irene was a gray-haired lady in her late seventies, and she answered her front door wearing a friendly smile and a frilly apron over her dress. Her home was filled with cat-shaped figurines crammed onto every shelf, mantelpiece and window ledge. The cushions on the sofas sported embroidered kitties and above her fireplace hung a photo gallery of cats of varying breeds and vintages. Irene was a devoted cat-lover, that was for sure.

"These have come straight out of the oven," she said, placing a tin of banana muffins on the coffee table. "Do help yourself, dear."

In between mouthfuls, I questioned Irene about her missing cat, Polly, who had been absent for over two days. It turned out that Irene's next-door neighbor, Cliff, was very unhappy that little Polly was using his vegetable patch as a litter box. He regularly complained about it over the fence.

"That filthy cat of yours has dug up my onions AGAIN!" he'd hollered one morning, brandishing his spade in anger.

"She's only doing what comes naturally, you old goat," she'd retorted. "Isn't it supposed to be good for your soil, anyway?"

When Polly had gone unexpectedly AWOL, Irene immediately assumed foul play on Cliff's part. Earlier in the week she'd objected to his liberal use of slug pellets—"You're trying to poison my Polly," she'd complained. The situation had become so heated that she'd called the police.

"D'you want to see what Polly looks like?" asked Irene, sliding a small, silver picture frame across her coffee table. Staring out from the photo was a well-fed, round-faced ginger-and-black cat with fierce lime-green eyes.

"Gosh, that looks like a cat who can take care of herself," I said.

"Yes, she gives as good as she gets," grinned Irene, "but she's got a soft nature, too, and is ever so friendly. She often sits on my front wall, meowing at the kids as they walk to school."

I noted how frail and vulnerable Irene looked and felt a pang of guilt that I hadn't thought this was important police business. To Irene, this was no trivial matter.

I polished off my second banana muffin and agreed to pay Cliff a visit. I needed to obtain his side of the story.

Cliff clearly hadn't expected to find a police officer on his doorstep. His face turned a deep shade of puce when I explained the reason for my call and he pulled out a handkerchief to dab the globules of sweat off his forehead.

He quickly claimed that Irene was overreacting and said that, while he was far from impressed with Polly's litter box habits, he'd threatened neither pet nor owner.

Cliff allowed me to search his back garden, more than half of which was taken up with his vegetable patch. I thoroughly explored the garage, greenhouse and potting shed. The only living things I encountered were beetles, spiders and wood lice.

His cheeks reddened again, however, when I requested access to his basement, the door to which opened directly onto the garden.

"Have you got a legal right to search?" he blustered.

"No, I haven't," I replied, "but if I arrested you on suspicion of cat theft, I'd have the power to search anywhere I wanted. So can I have a quick look, please?"

"Very well," he sighed, realizing that I wasn't going to be deterred. "Be my guest."

I unbolted the cellar door and, lo and behold, out of the darkness padded an angry-looking, dirt-encrusted tortoiseshell cat. It sprang over a tray of cat litter, shot out of the door and scaled the fence, no doubt heading for the welcoming arms of Irene, its owner.

I stared at Cliff, who scratched his head and shuffled from one foot to the other.

"Care to explain, Cliff?"

"That cat needed to be taught a lesson," he said. He explained that he'd only intended to keep Polly in the basement for a couple of days and that he'd provided her with ample food and water.

"I'm not going to get into any trouble, am I?" he asked anxiously.

"On this occasion, probably not," I replied, "but I do think you could have handled that better, Cliff. I'll do my best to smooth things over with Irene, but if the station receives one more call from her—just one—I'll be knocking on your door again, mark my words."

"I understand," he mumbled. "There'll be no repeat, I promise."

Years later, in May 1993 I was recruited to the Surrey Police Criminal Investigation Department. It was an incredibly proud moment for me. For years I'd dreamed of becoming a detective, and I was delighted to hang up my uniform and replace it with a smart blue suit.

I was fortunate to have a magnificent team of detectives at my disposal. Just as crucial, however, were the force's specially trained dogs. The vast majority were working cocker spaniels whose natural-born traits and attributes lent themselves perfectly to this unique role. Other than their innate intelligence, obedience and agility, what set these amazing dogs apart from other breeds was their phenomenal work rate and search stamina. This was backed up with a sense of smell which is 10,000 to 100,000 times stronger than a human's, which enabled them to follow a scent trail or decipher a specific odor that was undetectable to the nose of an average man or woman. Not only that, they were able to cover large or hard-to-reach areas much more quickly than a police officer. I came to realize that a cocker spaniel's hypersensitive nose was one of the finest tools in our crime unit, if not one of the most valuable assets in modern-day policing.

The canines—and their designated handlers—underwent extensive training at Surrey Police HQ for four months in order to receive their fit-for-practice certification. Each dog would go through an intensive scent-recognition program and be trained to identify unique odors. With each successful find, they were rewarded with play sessions involving their favorite toys.

The handlers clearly adored their canine companions and often formed close and loving bonds with them, despite the fact that the animals, technically, belonged to the force. Indeed, it was a well-known fact that most dog handlers would spend their entire careers on the dog section.

I had always had a great affection for cocker spaniels—I loved their spirit, loyalty and exuberance—so it was a delight to work with them in the crime unit.

Some dogs were more adept than others, I eventually realized, so I'd often request a specific handler if I knew that he'd be accompanied by a particular sniffer. A great example was Rainbow, an exceptionally talented dark brown cocker spaniel with yellow-amber eyes. She was Surrey Police's finest detection dog, with the best success rate, and she worked with a brilliant handler named John. Drugs-enforcement officers could search a house for hours—days, sometimes—and still fail to find any narcotics, due to clever concealment. But you couldn't hide them from a top dog's nose, and there weren't many noses better than Rainbow's.

Rainbow also reminded me very much of Tina, a black-and-white crossbreed whom I'd rescued a few years previously. She had been neglected and abused prior to being rescued and had understandably developed many behavioral problems. Once I'd showered her with love, care and attention, however, she grew into a fine pet, an energetic playmate and a wonderful companion. During my stint as a uniformed officer Tina would occasionally accompany me on a night shift, sitting quietly on the back seat during a stakeout or plain-clothes operation. I was heartbroken when she passed away—she died of a heart attack in 1990—and watching Rainbow brought all those happy memories flooding back.

One day after a job, while Rainbow was curled up on a sofa wedged between her handler, John, and me, we chatted about the sniffer dogs that he'd worked with through the years. I loved listening to the handlers' stories; they relished talking about their canine colleagues and often had some interesting tales to tell. I was always keen to absorb their knowledge and expertise—the whole concept of working with dogs intrigued me—and they willingly answered my questions, whether it was "What's the best dog for searches?" or "How many years can a dog work for?"

I had another question for John that day, though.

"I hope you don't mind me asking, but you've been in the force much longer than me. How come you're still a constable? How come you've never applied for promotion?"

His response was to the point, and from the heart.

"It's quite simple," he replied. "Had I gone for promotion and become a sergeant, I'd most likely have been taken off the dog section and would have had to give my dogs back. And I don't think I could have coped with that."

John gazed down at the sleeping dog and I detected a very slight lip wobble.

"I worship these animals, Sarge, whether it's Rainbow, or Sparky, or all those who've gone before. They're loyal, they're loving, and they're the best workmates you could ask for. Why would anyone in their right mind want to leave them, eh?"

A few years later, I was promoted again to detective inspector and was transferred to the Major Crimes Unit, which investigated organized crime and homicide. Unfortunately, this role meant that I had to attend endless meetings, training courses and seminars, which kept me away from operational policing. After realizing that my enthusiasm for the job had dimmed, in the spring of 2003 I decided to retire. I had been in the Royal Navy for eleven years, and the police force for fourteen. It was high time for a change.

I wanted to set up my own detective agency.

Prior to my departure, however, I wanted to carry out one final assignment with John and Rainbow. A couple of crooks had brazenly stolen the floodlights from the grounds of Guildford Cathedral and, a few weeks later, I'd received a tip about where the lights were. Naturally, I picked up the phone and called John.

"I've got a great job for you and Rainbow," I said. "I'll meet you on Ridgemount Road at 6 a.m."

It took our plucky little sniffer dog just thirty minutes to solve the case.

Since it was a bright and sunny morning—and knowing this might be the last time I saw my favorite dog-and-handler partnership—I suggested a walk to the top of Cathedral Hill. At the summit, John and I sat on a rickety old bench, gazing across the roads and rooftops of Guildford while Rainbow haphazardly played on the grass, snapping at bees and bluebottles.

"I'm really sorry that you're leaving, guv," said John, his eyes downcast. "Reckon we've done a pretty good job together."

"Having the best sniffer dog in Surrey certainly helps, John," I replied. "I often wonder how many successful finds she's had and how many lives she's saved."

"Countless," said John, keeping a close eye on Rainbow, "but if she gets stung by one of those bloomin' bees she's not going to be much use to me this week, is she?"

He reached into his pocket, pulled out a balding tennis ball and lobbed it down the hill, prompting Rainbow to abandon her bee-baiting and chase her favorite toy instead.

Suddenly, my colleague's radio crackled to life, relaying an urgent request for him to attend to an incident in Farnham. John's second sniffer dog, Sparky, was needed on the scene right away.

Having detected the familiar fizzle of radio interference, Rainbow pranced over and perched herself in front of John, panting heavily, her dark eyes dancing at the prospect of their next job.

"Sorry, girl, this one's not for you." He smiled, slotting his radio back in his top pocket before reattaching her leash.

"Well, I suppose I'd better be off then, guv," said John, shaking my hand. "I'll probably see you around, yeah?"

"No doubt you will," I replied, giving Rainbow's neck an affectionate little squeeze. "And keep up the good work, eh?"

I watched John jog down the hill toward his police van, Rainbow tight on his heels. Moments later they tore off along Cathedral Chase Road in a maelstrom of blue lights and screaming sirens.

While I was champing at the bit to kick off my new career as a private sleuth, I knew I'd dearly miss this dynamic duo. At the time I had no idea that soon I'd have my own canine partner-in-crime to work with.

3

FROM PRIVATE EYE TO
PET DETECTIVE

By the time I'd launched my own private-investigation business in autumn 2003, the role of the traditional detective had been revolutionized. Thanks to improvements in technology, gone were the days of shadowy men in raincoats peering around street corners and spying through holes in newspapers. Instead, professionals like me were more likely to be found scrutinizing footage from surveillance vehicles or examining someone's online footprint. Old-fashioned police-style detection techniques were still vital, of course—the finest private eyes were expert problem-solvers and critical thinkers—but the digital age had transformed the industry.

As time went by, many of my clients began to seek my help when their high-value pets and animals—exotic birds, hunting dogs or thoroughbred racehorses—went missing, or were subject to an ownership dispute.

Having established ourselves—albeit inadvertently—as the go-to detective agency for animal crime, I decided to set up a separate company and a distinct brand to run alongside my PI business.

On Monday, 3 October 2005, UK Pet Detectives was born. Launching our business on the eve of the Feast of St. Francis, the patron saint of animals, was wholly intentional on my part. I decided my first task was to recruit a new staff member to bolster our team and enhance our new service. Stefan, though an accomplished surveillance operative, wasn't a huge animal-lover and much preferred trailing devious fraudsters to tracing missing schnauzers.

I placed a small ad in the local newspaper, and in the space of a week, I'd received nearly a hundred applications, which I whittled down to half a dozen candidates. Sam was the last interviewee on my list and, within minutes of meeting her, I knew she was the right person for the role. She answered all my questions confidently and came across as a highly intelligent, witty and capable woman. Having managed a local animal rescue branch for a decade, she'd amassed a great knowledge and understanding of animal behavior and pet welfare, and her forte was people management. Her warmth and calmness were exactly what I was looking for, and I was thrilled when she accepted my job offer.

We set up our headquarters at Bramble Hill Farm in

West Sussex. This beautiful 500-acre estate was owned by an old friend of mine, James. Much of the land was leased to an alpaca farmer. When James had kindly offered me the use of a spacious converted barn for my fledgling business, I'd jumped at the chance.

"I tell you what, Colin," he'd said in his farmhouse kitchen, "I'll give you the barn rent-free, if you handle my estate security. Deal?"

"Deal," I'd replied without hesitation.

It was a crisp autumnal morning when Stefan, Sam and I first drove up to our new HQ, our moving van groaning with desks, computers and office equipment. James took some time to show us around the estate and, as we stood at its highest point, our T-shirts billowing in the stiff breeze, we couldn't help but marvel at the view. Velvety green hills rolled for as far as the eye could see, laced with blue-gray rivers and streams. Look left, and you saw pear and apple orchards next to fields of swaying ryegrass. Look right, and you saw deciduous forests bordering meadows of grazing alpacas. It was the sort of landscape you could gaze at for hours on end.

Bramble Hill Farm was also a renowned wildlife haven, explained James, who told us to expect to find foxes, rabbits and fallow deer loping past the office. The estate was a veritable paradise for fishermen and birdwatchers, too, its rivers teeming with trout, perch and crayfish, its skies filled with a multitude of raptors, finches and warblers.

"There's an old boar badger that wanders through the yard, too," he said, "but you'd better give him a wide berth because he's a grumpy old codger."

As well as its idyllic setting, our HQ had many practical and logistical advantages. The proximity of stables and paddocks—with robust locks and surveillance cameras—meant that UK Pet Detectives could provide animals with temporary or emergency sanctuary. We'd inevitably have to look after recovered dogs or horses for brief periods and the farm offered the necessary safety, shelter and privacy we needed. Our location couldn't have been more convenient. We were close to plenty of southeastern towns, villages and hamlets (most of which had large pet populations) and we were also within an hour's drive of London, where many of my existing PI clients lived and worked.

Sam and I got straight down to UKPD work, focusing our attention on four distinct areas: dog theft, lost or missing cats, equine-related crimes and bogus rescue centers and animal charities. We had received a number of reports from concerned individuals who'd donated to websites, only to discover that their money had been pocketed by crooks.

Sam helped UKPD to expand rapidly, and within nine months the number of pet-related calls to our office had tripled. During our first five years we recovered countless missing dogs: these included Baxter, a springer spaniel who'd become separated from his owner in the woods and had been stolen by a passing motorist, and Bertie, a Jack Russell terrier who'd been snatched from a horse stable. It had taken us just thirty minutes to recover Bertie, one of our fastest ever.

We also worked on some more outlandish cases, like the one initiated by a phone call from a lady who'd found our details online.

"My parrot's been stolen," she'd lamented, informing us that, following the disappearance of her beloved African gray parrot after a break-in, she'd received a tip-off that he was at an address over eighty miles away.

"But what you need to know," she'd explained, "is that Pongo's a talking parrot. He mimics stuff."

This lady wanted UKPD to drive to the address she'd received and eavesdrop in order to identify Pongo's cry and, hopefully, catch his captors red-handed.

But it turned out the bird was much closer to home. I had a call from a farmer who, having seen our MISSING PARROT posters, had realized that the "racing pigeon" resting beneath the eaves of his barn, screeching very strange sound bites, was something altogether more exotic. A raggedy-looking Pongo was carefully recaptured, then reunited with his very grateful owner.

Not every case could be solved, though. One winter we received a call from a panicked advertising executive who'd been staging a photoshoot for a famous design house. Their main prop was Montgomery, a five-foot-long albino ball python, who—to everyone's horror—had somehow escaped from its tank, where it had been left overnight.

Stefan and I turned up within the hour, having spoken to a reptile expert during our journey. He told me that ball pythons were so named because of the way they caught their prey; in their natural habitat, they'd curl up in burrows in order to ensnare shrews, gerbils and rabbits as they returned home.

"I'd advise that you look in any kitchens or bathrooms, since it'll probably have headed straight for water," he said, suggesting that I check pipes and wall cavities and telling me to hire an emergency plumber, which I did.

Stefan, the plumber and I arrived at the studio to find twenty terrified employees shivering on the pavement, refusing to go inside until Montgomery had been recaptured. Carrying the snake's empty aquarium, the three of us headed straight to the staff kitchen. We were in the process of rigging up our search equipment and dismantling the sink when a security guard strode in.

"Sorry, gents, but I'm afraid you'll have to leave," he said.

"What do you mean?" I replied. "You do know there's a snake on the loose?"

"Orders from on high, I'm afraid. The client is scared that the news is going to leak out, apparently, and they want to avoid any bad publicity before the ad campaign. So if you could exit the building, please, and just pop us an invoice in the mail."

We spent a few minutes arguing our case ("What's worse, the news getting out, or the snake?" I'd asked incredulously), but to no avail.

I never discovered what befell Montgomery the python. I'm hoping he was recovered that day and was quietly found a new home. That would have certainly been the best-case scenario.

While UKPD had always enjoyed incredible success recovering lost or stolen dogs, our ability to find cats had been, in comparison, fairly disappointing. Of all the cases we'd taken on, about thirty percent of the cats were found safe and well; more often than not, however, these pets had been missing for less than forty-eight hours, which usually meant that the search area was more confined and manageable.

A particularly memorable investigation, involving a woman named Suzie and a cat named Oscar, ended up having a profound effect upon me, and a pivotal effect upon my business. One morning in April 2012 I'd been feeding the chickens at Bramble Hill Farm when I felt my cell phone buzzing in my coat pocket. The woman on the end of the line frantically told me that her nine-month-old cat—a Burmilla—had gone missing in their tiny Hampshire village. After she mounted an unsuccessful search, her neighbor suggested she call my agency. In all my time as a pet detective, I'd rarely heard anyone so desperate for my help.

"Oscar's my world," Suzie had sobbed. "I'm worried sick, Mr. Butcher. I've hardly slept a wink and I need to find out what's happened to him."

Oscar, she explained, was a house cat who'd never before ventured outdoors. It turned out that, ten days previously, her husband had wedged open a kitchen window to rid the room of cooking fumes but had forgotten to shut it before bedtime. The following morning, Oscar had failed to pad upstairs for his usual snuggle and when Suzie had gone to investigate she'd noticed the open window and had gone into panic mode. Despite organizing a thorough search of the village and making numerous house-to-house inquiries, there'd not been a single sighting of him since.

As a general rule, I never took on cases relating to cats that had been missing for ten days or more. The likelihood of recovering them was significantly reduced by that stage, and I wasn't in the business of raising my clients' hopes—or charging them—for what was often a lost cause. But this woman's voice sounded so sad that it compelled me to lend my assistance, and at seven o'clock the next morning I found myself knocking on her front door.

Suzie, in her late thirties with a kind face and a mop of brown curls, lived in the village of East Meon with her husband, Mike. Over a cup of tea, she answered my questions about Oscar. I approached missing-pet investigations meticulously and forensically—just like I'd done earlier in my career, when I'd tackled missing-persons cases for Surrey Police—and learned as much as I could about the animal's character, health and routine. This enabled me to compile a detailed profile and ensured that I didn't waste valuable time searching in the wrong location or at the wrong time of day. The more Suzie and I chatted, however, the more I understood the true extent of her despair. She had been through a lot in the past two years, having lost both of her parents. Her husband, Mike, had been racking his brains to think of something to help her feel better.

"So that's when he came home from work with a kitten." Suzie smiled and unpinned a photograph of Oscar from her kitchen bulletin board before handing it to me. "Nothing could fill the void of losing my parents, of course, but he thought I might like a little companion."

"He's a beauty," I said, staring at his enormous mint-green eyes.

Suzie had been somewhat skeptical—she'd never owned a cat before—but when Oscar arrived, with his marbled brown coat and his snow-white whiskers, she was smitten. As she'd lifted him from his carrying case, he'd immediately begun to purr and had raised his front legs, gently pawing at the sleeves of her cardigan.

Her new friend would sit on her lap as she typed, rub against her ankles as she made lunch and curl up beside her at night, like a big, fluffy comma. Whenever Suzie felt sad, her feline friend seemed to detect it, nuzzling closer into her neck or purring with increased volume. He also had a habit of pouncing on her slippers and nibbling at her toes, which would send her into fits of giggles. Much to Mike's delight, Suzie and Oscar soon became inseparable.

"He sounds like a wonderful cat," I said, prompting my client to nod forlornly.

Once I had gathered the required information, I prepared to commence the search. I promised to keep her posted about any significant developments.

"Thanks, Colin," she said, blinking back tears as she handed me a wad of MISSING CAT leaflets that she had printed. "I just want my Oscar back."

THE CATALYST FOR CHANGE

Finding this missing cat was crucial. I opted to begin the search in Suzie's garden. The two-meter drop from the kitchen window to the patio would have prevented Oscar from jumping back into the house; I'd investigated a few similar cases and reckoned that, in a quest for safety, security and warmth, he'd probably sought refuge close by. Given the lack of confirmed sightings, it was highly likely that this was a case of accidental lock-in and that the cat had most probably become trapped in an outbuilding. With the help of some cooperative neighbors and shop owners, I gained entry to as many gardens, sheds and garages as I could. It proved to be a time-consuming affair, since many of the stone-built, thatched-roofed cottages in this genteel village had long, snaking driveways threading through large, sprawling gardens. More frustratingly, when I finally reached the doorstep, I'd often find that the occupants weren't home, meaning that some potential hideaways remained unsearched.

By mid-afternoon I'd drawn a blank—there was simply no trace of Oscar—and as time passed my hopes of finding him began to fade. Every minute mattered when a cat had been absent for such a long period of time, as I knew only too well, and I braced myself for a tough conversation with Suzie.

One particular property continued to pique my interest, though. Occupying the largest plot in East Meon, this large converted farmhouse boasted a swimming pool to the east, a tennis court to the west and—more pertinently—a spacious shed to the rear.

I had already visited the house twice that morning, but on both occasions my knocks on the door had gone unanswered. However, as I began to make tracks to Suzie's—it must have been about four o'clock—I noticed a sporty blue BMW parked in the driveway. I jogged up and rapped the shiny brass knocker, and crossed my fingers. After a minute or so, the door creaked open and I was faced with a fair-haired fifty-something woman dressed in skinny jeans and a leather jacket.

"Good afternoon." I smiled, introducing myself and holding up a leaflet. "I'm searching for a missing cat, Oscar, and I'm wondering if I could have a quick peek in your shed?"

The lady fixed me with a glacial stare.

"It's a pool house, not a shed," she replied. "And, in any case, there's no need for you to go inside. I've seen all the posters around the village, and I've searched it myself. There's no cat in there, I can assure you."

I wasn't convinced. Thirty years spent in the police force or as a private detective had equipped me with an array of finely tuned interpersonal skills, and my built-in lie detector was bleeping like crazy. The woman had turned her back toward the shed while talking to me, had provided me with information I hadn't asked for and, most crucially, had broken eye contact at the precise moment she'd mentioned searching the place. I was convinced that she hadn't been near it for weeks, which made me all the more determined to gain access.

"I'd really like to have a quick look, if you don't mind . . . ," I asked politely.

The woman defensively folded her arms and slowly shook her head.

"It'll only take five minutes, I promise," I added hastily, while flashing her a friendly smile. "Oscar's owner is distraught and just needs to know what's happened to him one way or another. I'd be ever so grateful."

Her mood seemed to thaw momentarily and, with a resigned sigh, she headed off down her hallway, reappearing with a silver key dangling from her forefinger.

"But I shall be coming with you," she said, arching her eyebrows, "and you'd better be as quick as you say."

She opened the shed and ushered me in. To the right, illuminated by a shaft of sunlight, was a large plastic box full of pool accessories: deflated rafts, snorkels and flippers. A metal shelving unit on the shadier, left-hand side of the shed—sorry, pool house—housed some terra-cotta plant pots and some loosely stacked hanging baskets, the latter separated by pale green jute liners.

"As you can see," said the woman, returning to her icy self, "there's no cat in here."

Suddenly, out of the corner of my eye, I noticed one of the hanging baskets wobbling slightly. Then I heard a faint rustling, accompanied by a feeble mewing sound. Within seconds, a tiny paw had poked itself out of the wire basket. At first sight his fur appeared to be black, and my heart sank, but as the animal clambered out of his dark corner, there was no mistaking that distinctive coat and those huge green eyes. Oscar.

Looking gaunt and bedraggled, he took a couple of faltering steps before collapsing at my feet. I carefully scooped him up and—without exchanging a single word with the woman, who was probably cringing in embarrassment—I cradled Oscar in my arms and exited the garden. Apart from a half-hearted claw at my fleece, the cat offered little resistance. The poor fella was far too frail to sense any kind of stranger-danger.

I walked over to my car and gently placed the trembling kitty on the passenger seat, tenderly brushing away the cobwebs from his matted fur. I slowly drove over to Suzie's, calling ahead to inform her I'd found her cat but stressing that we needed to take him to the vet immediately. She was waiting for us at her front gate, anxiously clasping her hands to her chest.

"My Oscar!" she gasped as she opened the passenger door.

For her, it was both the best-case scenario and the worst. While she was utterly overjoyed to see her precious pet alive—he'd survived, I reckoned, by licking the condensation off the shed windows—she was greatly distressed by his frail, skeletal appearance. His sky-high temperature, bone-dry nose and glassy eyes confirmed that we were dealing with a very ill cat who needed urgent medical attention.

I dropped them off at the vet—a concerned nurse was already waiting at the entrance. My head was pounding as I drove home. I was angry at the woman who had failed to search her shed and furious at myself for not finding Oscar earlier. I felt terrible that I couldn't have done more for Suzie; seeing her so upset had been hard enough, but suspecting that there was worse to come left me feeling so helpless.

Suzie called me with an update the next morning. The vet had diagnosed severe dehydration.

His only chance of long-term survival was a swift transfer to a specialist treatment center in London. The vet couldn't offer any guarantees that this course of action would work, however. Suzie was adamant, though.

"It's going to cost me a fortune, Colin, but he's worth it," she said. "I promise I'll keep you posted."

When she rang me for the second time that weekend, her quivering voice told me all I needed to know. Oscar didn't make it.

I tried to say the right things, and when she couldn't talk anymore, Mike took over the conversation.

"It wasn't the happy ending she wanted, Colin, but Suzie's so grateful for your help," he said. "Had you not found him, she wouldn't have been able to say a proper goodbye."

I put down the phone, leaned back in my chair and gazed out the window.

Suzie had put her trust and faith in me and, despite my best efforts, I'd failed her. Had my tactics been more effective and strategic, poor Oscar could have been recovered hours earlier, and that might well have made all the difference. I needed to find a more efficient way to search, without compromising on quality. *You can't let this happen again, Colin*, I said to myself. *Something needs to change.*

It was time to put my long-standing idea into practice. It was time to test my trailblazing concept once and for all.

It was time, I realized, to finally find myself a cat-detection dog.

In the meantime, however, I decided that UKPD had to start studying cat behavior in much finer detail. Sam, who knew just how devastated I'd been following Oscar's case, was in full agreement.

"Now that we're not handling as many dog thefts, there's no reason why we shouldn't devote more of our resources to cats," she said one afternoon.

"We need to get up close and personal with cats. We need to watch what they get up to, where they go, who they interact with, why they go missing."

My colleague was spot-on. Our results hadn't been great, and there was surely more work that we could do to understand a cat's mindset and to track its movements. Over the course of that evening we hatched a plan, a far-reaching strategy aimed at equipping ourselves with as much knowledge and information as possible.

For the next few weeks we pored over numerous cat-behavior books, studied reams of academic papers and watched a wealth of films and documentaries. Stefan kept the private-investigation side of my business going nicely.

This initiative, we decided, would be an innovative, groundbreaking experiment. To provide us with real insight into cat behavior, we'd identify some willing cat owners and, with their consent, affix small GPS tracking devices to their pets' collars. We would then monitor the data, which would aim to address some pertinent questions: Where did cats go when they left their homes, and what did they get up to?

First and foremost, we had to choose a decent location for our research.

"Why don't we do it in Shamley Green?" said Sam.

"Yeah, why not?" I replied. "I think it'd be perfect."

Quintessentially English, it boasted large fields and a variety of quaint shops and eateries, including the renowned Speckledy Hen Café. Crucially, it also had an unusually high density of cats, something I'd noticed while working there on previous investigations. Everywhere I'd turned, I'd seen cats staring out of windows, sitting on doorsteps or moseying along the pavement.

The next step was to recruit some volunteers, so Sam and I displayed posters in shop windows, delivered flyers to local households and posted messages on local social media sites.

ARE YOU A CAT OWNER? they stated. UK PET DETECTIVES IS SEEKING A BETTER UNDERSTANDING OF FELINE BEHAVIOR AND WE'D LOVE YOU TO GET INVOLVED . . .

Ten interested parties made contact, and we eventually slimmed it down to three. We purposely chose some largish cats who could easily carry the GPS devices on their collars: Monty, a docile silver Maine coon; Shamley, a female tabby who'd lived in the village for ten years; and Branson, a longhaired ginger tom named after a rather successful businessman who'd once resided nearby.

"Let's hope it's all worthwhile," said Sam, smiling on day one, crossing her fingers as we set off to the owners' houses, where we'd show them how to attach the cat trackers. If things went as planned, we'd retrieve some useful and valuable information.

What we didn't realize was that we'd unwittingly chosen the three laziest cats in Shamley Green. A week or so later—and much to our disappointment—the data analysis at UKPD HQ showed that these silly kitties had hardly moved a muscle. Shamley, the most active of the trio, would plod to the bottom of the garden each morning, where she'd sit on the shed roof for a few hours, sunning herself and guarding her territory. After doing her business in a neighbor's garden, she'd then return to her kitchen for lunch, have a snooze on the sofa, then repeat this whole eat-poop-sleep cycle in the afternoon.

For our project's purposes, this lack of activity was deeply unsatisfactory. But then we had a stroke of luck. A local magazine editor asked to interview us about UKPD. I agreed and mentioned our project with the intention of attracting more participants. Within days of publication we'd recruited a dozen more volunteers.

At long last, we began to collect some fantastic data. Our new cohort of cats was infinitely more lively and, as Sam and I observed the film footage and analyzed the GPS range maps, we began to piece together some marvelous information. We learned an awful lot about cats' day-to-day behavior, habits and movements and, critically, the circumstances that led them to migrate or go missing. Some cats, we noted, reacted adversely to a change within the household—the arrival of a new baby, perhaps, or even a room being redecorated— and others were driven from their usual territory by an aggressive cat encroaching on their home or garden.

Some of the most remarkable cat's-eye-view footage captured the activities of so-called "intruder" cats, who habitually snuck into neighboring properties to seek food and shelter. We watched intently as a plump British Blue cat named Norman sat at the end of his driveway every morning, his eyes focused on the neighbors' house across the way. This couple left for work at 6:30 a.m. each day and no sooner had they departed than Norman would stroll across the road, enter the kitchen via a cat door, pilfer some of their own cat's food and pad around their house like he owned the place!

About half an hour before the couple was due home, Norman reemerged from the back door, ambled over the road and rejoined his "parent" household. Both sets of owners were astonished, but amused, when I played back this revealing footage.

"No wonder he's so tubby!" Norman's owner exclaimed.

The cat's routine continued, although Norman's owner seems to have provided extra food for him at the neighbors' house.

Not all intruder cats were so docile. A few weeks into our project we noticed a slightly unkempt, longhaired, gray-and-white cat, who seemed to be entering a multitude of houses. He had the telltale swagger of an unneutered tom and was making a real menace of himself. He muscled his way into cat doors or open windows and proceeded to ambush other cats, gobble up their food and, for good measure, spray his urine up the walls in an attempt to claim his territory. Sam and I nicknamed him Titan.

One unfortunate family unwittingly locked this formidable cat in their utility room, having accidentally adjusted the settings on their cat door so that he'd been able to enter, but not exit. When they returned home late after a day trip, they were confronted with a trashed room and a livid cat. Titan had not taken kindly to being locked in and had gone berserk; the window blinds were hanging off their hinges, the contents of a laundry basket had been shredded and the place stank of cat pee. They couldn't open the back door quickly enough, breathing a huge sigh of relief when Titan fled into the night.

Despite his destructive and dominant tendencies, over time I became strangely fond of Titan. I used to enjoy tracking him as he patrolled the village—I could often pinpoint his whereabouts via the motion-sensitive cameras. Was Titan a feral cat who had always lived in the wild? Or was he a stray cat who'd once had a home or perhaps still had an owner somewhere? I decided to investigate.

I plastered dozens of DO YOU KNOW THIS CAT? posters around the area, in the hope that any owner would recognize him. Then, in order to build a comprehensive profile of Titan, I interviewed all the neighbors who'd reported sightings of him and analyzed footage from our array of cameras. He was frequenting five separate households, all of which owned cats that he could either fight with, mate with, or—very rarely—socialize with. There was only one property he visited on a daily basis, though, a neat bungalow owned by Valerie, an amiable woman in her late sixties. She was a committed cat-lover—she owned Max, an elderly Burmese male—and had developed a fondness for Titan, who'd regularly pop in for a snack or a snooze.

"Funnily enough, I've never had any problems with him," she said, when I'd described Titan's unruly behavior. "He always seems pretty settled here, and Max is too decrepit to cause him any bother. In fact, I'd say they get on really well. He's quite the softie when he wants to be."

Valerie was even considering adopting Titan. I gently explained that I felt it was my duty to try and trace his background, which might allow me to return him to his rightful owner—if he had one—and to restore some stability to his life. He also needed to be neutered for his health and the health of the cats he encountered.

With all that in mind, Valerie allowed me to set up a humane cat trap in her kitchen one evening—basically, a large, airy plastic-coated crate with some food as bait—so I could contain him with ease. Then I'd take him to the vet for a health check, and to determine if he was microchipped.

Valerie called me at eight o'clock the following morning.

"I think you need to come over, Colin," she whispered. "I've got a rather bad-tempered cat in my kitchen."

Titan was none too pleased to see me, hissing angrily and swaying his bottlebrush tail as I advanced toward him. Luckily, I managed to calm him down with a handful of cat treats and a few soothing words and was able to transfer him to a much comfier carrying case.

Just as we left for the vet, I received a call from Sam. It seemed a lady named Mrs. Lewis had left a message the previous evening, stating that she'd seen my poster on a noticeboard and claiming that Titan belonged to her.

"She says his real name is Milo," said Sam, "and she reckons he went missing from Bramley six months ago."

The village was only a ten-minute drive from Shamley Green and I knew it well.

"Right, okay," I replied. "I'll drop the big fella off at the vet and I'll go and pay her a visit."

Mrs. Lewis, a mother of two in her thirties, greeted me at the doorstep and led me into her kitchen. She rummaged in a drawer and produced a photograph of a brawny gray cat—it was unmistakably Titan—before telling me how distraught her children had been when he'd gone missing and how they'd given up hope of ever seeing him again. She also explained that his disappearance had coincided with one of their three female cats giving birth to a litter of six kittens.

"That's actually a classic trigger for a cat to go missing," I said, explaining how cats were extremely

Titan, aka Milo, who was missing for six months,
after he was reunited with his owners

sensitive to changes to their environment and how all the fuss and upheaval in the household could have caused him to migrate to a new territory. Mrs. Lewis told me that most of the kittens had been adopted and that the eldest female cat had passed away.

"Suffice to say that it's much calmer and quieter here these days," she said, "so we'd love to have Milo back."

I offered Mrs. Lewis a couple of nuggets of advice: first and foremost, it was high time to get the cat neutered and, secondly, she should try to curb the number of cats in the household, because that had probably triggered his disappearance.

Titan, aka Milo, was soon reunited with his elated family, bringing an absorbing investigation to a satisfying close.

I bade farewell to Titan and made my way back to Bramble Hill Farm. While I was pleased to see him back with his family, I couldn't help but wonder how long willful, wandering Milo would remain there.

Our project had been an incredibly worthwhile exercise. Invaluable data recorded by our trackers and cameras had enabled us to obtain a fresh insight into cat behavior—their secret lives—and had cast new light upon the issue of feline migration. Armed with this newfound knowledge, UK Pet Detectives was able to take on more cases of lost and missing cats and our recovery success rate soared to over sixty percent. For me, however, that still wasn't high enough. I couldn't bear our occasional failures, and I knew I needed to shift things into high gear.

5

A PIONEERING PROJECT

The seed of my cat-detection-dog idea had been sown during my teenage years in 1970s England. I'd spent my childhood in Malaysia and Singapore—my father was an engineering officer in the Royal Navy—and my family had returned to the UK when I was twelve. My passion for the outdoors had started in the rainforests of the Far East and it continued when we relocated to England. I loved being outside and observing local nature and wildlife, no matter what it was.

My parents and grandparents were huge natural-science lovers, too, and actively encouraged my hobby. Christmas and birthday presents always seemed to bring new reference guides. And I'd regularly bring home creatures that I caught during field trips, such as newts, lizards and grass snakes.

"You've had them two days, son, best take them back now," Dad would suggest, as a selection of small insects and amphibians writhed around in homemade habitats. "They belong in the wild, son, not in your bedroom."

My elder brother, David, and I spent many school vacations in a nearby sheep-farming area with a very good friend of my grandfather's—Alec—a self-proclaimed "countryman" in his late sixties who kept an eye on the farmers' land and their livestock. Alec would drive us in a battered, bottle-green jeep, its beige canvas roof pulled on or peeled off depending on the weather. The vehicle had a distinctive smell of dog, sheep and pipe smoke; Alec's tobacco had a honeyed, pine-cone tang, and David and I would come home reeking of it.

Bouncing around in the back of the truck would be a couple of black-and-white collies—the most skillful and traditional of sheepdogs—who'd help to corral the animals and rescue them from perilous situations. Sometimes Alec would receive a call to say that a sheep had fallen down a quarry, for example.

"Ready for action, lads?" he'd ask, our adrenaline pumping as we squeezed into the passenger seat. "A daft old ram's got himself stuck in a stile, so we'll need to go and untangle him."

I worshipped Alec. His knowledge of the local area was unrivaled (he knew every hill, dale and dirt track) and no one understood collies like him. He doted on those dogs—he'd talk to them with such tenderness, as if they were his own sons—and they repaid him with their utmost trust and loyalty. Alec worked his dogs hard, but he also loved them deeply; it was a dynamic that I found mesmerizing.

Throughout my childhood, we had a procession of pets including dogs, cats, hamsters and mice (they were smuggled into the house without my parents' knowledge and hidden in my sock drawer, where they used to escape with annoying frequency). My mom and dad developed a serious soft spot for shih tzus, and I'd often come home from school to discover another cute golden-coated puppy bounding around the back garden, picked up that afternoon from our local branch of the SPCA. My parents always took on rescue dogs—for them, it was a matter of principle—and would never visit specialist breeders or pet shops.

"Every dog deserves a second chance," Mom would say, scooping up the latest addition to our family and giving him an affectionate nuzzle.

Gemini, a silver-and-white shih tzu rescue, was so clever that he recognized the names of his favorite toys when we called them out. He also got along with our resident cat, Mitzy, a confident and incredibly affectionate two-year-old tortoiseshell. The furry friends would snuggle up together in Gemini's fleecy dog bed. Mitzy was an adorable little thing, with sage-green eyes and a distinctive snow-white coat splotched with black and orange. In between her many naps—like most cats, she slept for up to sixteen hours a day—she had a habit of following me around the house, meowing for my attention. I was more than happy to oblige; she clearly favored me over my three siblings, and Mom and Dad were often too busy to run up and down the stairs with a catnip mouse.

One wintry Saturday in November, Mitzy vanished into thin air. We thought it was strange that she hadn't surfaced for lunch—she loved her food and had a plump little belly to show for it—and there was still no sign of her the next morning. David and I organized the family search party, scouring our back garden, rummaging through hedges and, when that came to nothing, knocking on neighbors' doors. We spent an entire Sunday evening drawing MISSING CAT posters with our colored pencils, then attached them to lamp posts and tree trunks.

"Don't worry, boys, she'll probably return of her own accord," said my mother. But as the hours turned into days—and the outdoor temperatures plummeted—my hope waned. Gemini seemed to sense our worry. He, too, appeared more stressed and anxious than usual, running haphazardly around the house, stopping occasionally to scratch, whimper and look up at us dolefully.

"Poor Gemini," I lamented, giving him a big bear hug. "He's missing Mitzy as much as we are."

The following Thursday, almost a week after our cat had gone AWOL, we were all watching TV when Gemini started crouching in the corner, whining and pawing at the carpet.

"I wish he'd stop doing that," grumbled my mom. "We only laid that a month ago and it's already threadbare."

Over the noise of the TV, I became distracted by a sudden sound from across the room.

"Hey, I'm sure I just heard a meow," I said, sitting bolt upright. "Turn the volume down, Dad."

We all listened intently for a couple of minutes, but heard nothing.

"It was probably Suzi Quatro hitting a high note," grinned Dad, whacking the sound back up.

Moments later a loud, distinctive meow emanated from the corner of the room and a light bulb went on in my head. Our clever shih tzu, with his superior scenting and hearing skills, was indicating that our cat was down below. That's why Gemini was moaning and scratching. The poor dog had probably been trying to alert us for days and we just hadn't read the signs. "*MITZY'S UNDER THE FLOORBOARDS!*" I screeched, dashing over to the corner. "That's why Gemini's been acting so weird."

Mom sprang up from the sofa, put her hands on her hips and glared at my father.

"This is *your* fault," she hissed.

"What d'you mean?" replied my startled dad.

"You took up the kitchen floor last weekend, didn't you? The cat must've sneaked in when you weren't looking."

My father had indeed been replacing some crumbling water pipes the previous weekend, and Mitzy had evidently slipped in before he'd nailed the floorboards back down.

"But I hardly moved from the kitchen," said Dad somewhat sheepishly. "And surely I would have noticed her—"

"Clearly not, Geoff," responded my mom indignantly. "You'd better go and get your toolbox. That poor little thing needs to see the light of day."

Chaos ensued for the next hour as we heard an agitated Mitzy scampering off in different directions, her subterranean movements being closely tracked by Gemini, his ears pointing north, his snout pointing south. My father, armed with a claw hammer, ripped back carpets and wrenched up floorboards as David and I poked flashlights through the gaps, cajoling our cat with cries of "Mitzy, *ch-ch-ch* . . . Mitzy, *ch-ch-ch* . . ."

Mom cradled my baby brother, Rian, in her arms, watching in horror as her house was torn apart.

A growling Gemini indicated that Mitzy had reached a cul-de-sac beneath the downstairs bathroom. As our dog spun around in excitement, Dad carefully edged up a floorboard and, after a few tense moments, out crept a befuddled, bedraggled little cat, encrusted with dirt and grime and sporting a noticeably slimmer tummy. Rian's gleeful yelp of delight, followed by a peal of laughter, said it all. Gemini had found Mitzy.

Watching my brainy dog find my beloved cat was one of the most amazing things I'd ever seen and, unbeknownst to me, had imprinted a grand idea onto my psyche. It would be another four decades before I fully explored its true potential.

As we approached the winter of 2014, I felt the time had come to launch the second phase of my cat-detection plan. A specialist scent-recognition dog would not only complement our project but would also complete my team, enhance our service, and—most important—increase our chances of finding these missing pets. This would in turn bring joy and relief to their owners and, hopefully, avoid tragic outcomes like poor Oscar, which continued to haunt me. I was utterly convinced it was a viable concept; if a police canine could be taught to detect a specific drug or firearm, I saw no reason why a dog couldn't be trained to isolate the odor of a particular cat. In my mind, it was eminently doable.

I knew that I wouldn't be able to complete the project alone and that I'd need some expert help along the way. A good friend had once advised me that, in order for a great idea to work, "You first need the know-how, and then you need the know-who," and it was with that simple equation in mind that Sam and I got started. Although I had vast experience with dogs—I'd always had them in my life and I'd owned and trained a succession of rescues—I lacked expertise in the science of canine behavior and scent recognition.

Throughout 2014, I studied these subjects, reading hundreds of academic books and papers and watching countless documentaries on television and on YouTube.

Sam and I would spend hours discussing everything we'd learned, which gave us much food for thought.

"Just think, Colin, if all goes to plan, you could have yourself the UK's first cat-detection dog," I remember her once saying. "How brilliant would that be?"

I took advantage of my contacts book and client list, too, first, to judge whether there was anyone in the region who could help me find and train a specialist dog (or point me in the direction of someone who could), and, second, to find out what people thought of my idea. What I hadn't expected, however, was to hit a brick wall of negativity.

A contact of mine kindly put me in touch with a gun-dog breeder, but when I paid her a visit she quickly shut me down.

"I can't see that ever working," she sneered, "and if it is such a good idea, don't you think an established dog trainer would have done it by now?"

Okay, maybe it's never been done before, I remember thinking as I walked back to my car, *but that doesn't mean it can't be done.*

Other dog trainers didn't bother to return my calls and emails, and a Kennel Club official rudely implied that I didn't possess the expertise to take on a project like this. Another so-called expert took great pleasure in telling me that sniffer dogs were better equipped to search for people rather than cats, since humans were more heavy-footed and therefore easier to trace.

"Felines are hunters, Mr. Butcher, so they creep around very quietly and don't tend to disturb the ground," he said, shaking his head condescendingly. "And, because they're covered in fur, they don't shed as many skin cells as we do. For those reasons, cats would be very, very hard to locate."

"Well, let's just say I respectfully beg to differ," I replied, biting my tongue.

The same individual also questioned whether a

scent-recognition dog would be able to pinpoint one particular cat within a community of hundreds, since he assumed that they all "had the same smell." My extensive reading—together with the findings from my research project—had already convinced me otherwise.

I even contacted Surrey Police's dog-training center, hoping they might be interested in a PR-friendly joint venture. I would fund the specialist tuition for the sniffer dog and the force could take the credit for the outcome. The sergeant laughed at me.

"I can't say that missing cats are a priority of ours," he said, barely able to hide his amusement, "so I really don't think it's something we'd be interested in."

To him, I was probably some deluded pet detective touting a hare-brained idea that might damage the police force's professional reputation.

Unusually for me, there weren't any animals roaming around my place at that point in time. I was still mourning the loss of three beloved rescue dogs in the space of eighteen months—Tess the German shepherd and my two rottweilers, Max and Jay—and I'd decided to have an extended break from pet ownership.

I occasionally fostered animals as part of my UK Pet Detectives work. Invariably, they were recovered stolen dogs whose owners were untraceable or abandoned cats who were waiting to be adopted. It was when I'd provided temporary housing for Bracken the springer spaniel that I realized my girlfriend, Sarah, wasn't the world's greatest dog-lover. Given the choice, she much preferred cats. Painstakingly tidy and immaculately groomed, my girlfriend, it seemed, didn't take kindly to doggies and their dirt.

"Ugh, Colin, there's mud everywhere . . . ," she'd wailed when Bracken and I had returned from a soggy walk in the woods, leaving a trail of mucky paw- and footprints along the hallway.

"And there's dog hair all over the kitchen, for goodness' sake!" she'd exclaimed. "It's revolting . . ."

While Sarah had known about my cat-detection-dog plans from day one, I think, deep down, she'd doubted it would ever come to fruition. After my failure to recruit the Surrey Police she kept her feelings well hidden.

"You're not throwing in the towel, are you, Colin?" she asked.

"No chance. If anything, it's making me more determined," I replied. "I just need to find somebody who believes in me, and who believes in my idea. They must be out there somewhere."

They were indeed, most notably in the guise of a dog-lover named Anna.

While my "pet project" ate up much of my spare time, I still had to manage my private-detective agency, and I continued to handle animal-related cases and crimes. One afternoon, I received a call from a woman asking if I could possibly investigate the suspicious death of her Welsh terrier, Molly. A well-regarded dog trainer and canine expert, Anna had relocated from central London to give Molly, to whom she was absolutely devoted, a better quality of life. The dog had been diagnosed with cancer a few months previously and Anna felt that the fresher air and calmer environment would boost her pooch's health, and perhaps prolong its life. But an incident with an untrustworthy dog sitter seemed to have led to Molly's untimely demise.

Despite a long, intricate investigation, there wasn't enough evidence for a civil or criminal prosecution. But my client was satisfied to have obtained a few answers to her questions and to have some kind of closure.

"I'll never, ever forget Molly—she was my best friend—but now I feel I can finally let her rest in peace," she told me.

Anna and I went on to become firm friends. She was wonderful company—I loved her constant stream of dog anecdotes—and, when she moved back to London, we regularly met up for coffee. It was during one such get-together, in a Notting Hill café, that I raised the subject of a cat-detection dog.

"Listen, Anna, I've got this idea," I said. "Everyone else seems to think it's some kind of pipe dream and that I've totally lost the plot, but I'd really value your opinion."

Not only did my friend think it was a fabulous concept, she was also confident she knew an organization that could assist. She had once worked with a charity called Medical Detection Dogs, whose staff were doing pioneering work with specialist scent-recognition canines. They had successfully trained a number of medical-alert assistance dogs. These amazing creatures used their ultra-sensitive noses to detect minuscule changes in an individual's personal odor, which enabled them to spot certain warning signs. If one of

Molly relaxing with one of the cats she found after a training search at MDD

these dogs was paired with a person living with Type 1 diabetes, for example, it would be trained to sense dangerously high or low blood sugar levels and would alert the patient to this medical event by either jumping up or licking, or both. Similar dogs assisted people with severe food allergies.

"These dogs are phenomenal, Colin," remarked Anna. "They don't just change lives, they save them."

According to my friend, MDD was also conducting on-site trials with specialist bio-detection dogs. Astonishingly enough, these animals were being trained to detect certain cancers by odor alone—via samples of breath, urine and skin swabs—the hope being that, one day, they could assist with the clinical screening of the disease. For this innovative research, the charity had recruited working breeds that possessed excellent noses and a natural hunting instinct—such as Labradors and cocker spaniels—and had devoted between six and eight months to train them. All the dogs lived in the homes of staff or local volunteer fosterers (never in kennels) and were loved and cared for as part of a family.

"MDD could be just what you're looking for," said Anna. "I can't promise anything, obviously, but I can certainly set up a meeting."

I met Dr. Claire Guest and Rob Harris—the driving forces behind Medical Detection Dogs—on Wednesday, 25 September 2015. Claire was the charity's chief executive officer. Rob had trained a multitude of dogs to detect all manner of things, ranging from dry rot in historical buildings to bedbug infestations in hotels and illegally trafficked ivory.

"It's all about taking what a dog does naturally and honing it into a unique skill," said Rob when I quizzed him about his impressive career portfolio. "What's great, though," he added, "is that the majority of these dogs don't view their work as a chore. They see it as a fabulous game of hide-and-seek that they absolutely love playing and which they get rewarded for."

They both listened intently as I presented my case, with Anna at my side for moral support. When I finished speaking and closed down the PowerPoint, they glanced at each other and nodded.

"In principle, I definitely think it's something we could help you with," said Claire. "It's an excellent concept, Colin, and—if done properly—I reckon it could be potentially groundbreaking."

I couldn't believe what I was hearing. It was a eureka moment for me. I felt like leaping up and dancing around the room, and it took all my effort to remain seated.

"I think it's a really exciting challenge," Claire went

on, "and, as an animal-lover myself, I really admire the reasons behind it. A dog that finds cats . . . I mean, what's not to like?"

She also explained that, if things went as planned, they'd consider bringing in a contact of theirs—Astrid, a scent-matching expert from Chile—for the dog's laboratory-based training. They told me that Astrid had just finished working on a special assignment with the German police force that had involved training sniffer dogs to match scenes of crimes with specific offenders.

"Astrid is astoundingly good at what she does; in fact, I'd say she's among the best in the world," said a smiling Rob. "I'm sure she'd love to work with us."

This was music to my ears. Like Astrid's training technique, my specialist detection dog would also be expected to distinguish one-off scents. Each search would involve the recognition of a cat's unique individual odor. I had a feeling that Astrid's expertise would prove to be vital.

As we wrapped up the meeting I felt like pinching myself. At last, and thanks to Anna's intervention, I'd met some brilliant people with "can-do" attitudes who'd actually bought into my idea. I had clicked with a group of pioneering professionals who were prepared to help me push boundaries and overcome hurdles in order to create something fresh and innovative.

"So, are we in agreement?" I asked somewhat cautiously.

"Yes, I think we are," replied Claire. "Let's make this happen."

Now that I'd joined forces with MDD, it was time to make an important decision. We needed to pinpoint the ideal breed for our project. Over the years, I'd encountered working dogs of all descriptions, not only within the police force and the pet-detective arena but also by visiting various field trials, game shoots and county shows in the southeast region. I was forever picking the brains of owners and breeders so that I could build up a picture of my ultimate working dog.

My research was based on two key questions. First, what would be the most effective and efficient dog from my perspective? Second—and crucially—what would be the best dog in the eyes of a missing (and possibly traumatized) cat?

It was imperative that I find a dog that had a natural-born instinct to search. Claire had suggested the vizsla breed—a Hungarian pointer with incredible air-scenting ability—but I thought it would be too big; our dog needed to be small enough to squeeze itself into confined spaces. It also needed the energy and endurance to embark upon lengthy, time-consuming assignments, which would often involve an element of travel.

Trainability was a key factor, too. If this dog was going to be taught highly technical skills at MDD, it was essential that it was extremely alert, intelligent and quick-witted. Personality-wise, our ideal breed needed to be sociable and obedient in order to interact happily with different types of people within a variety of settings and scenarios.

As far as the cat's-eye view, the last thing we needed was an overly noisy dog or an animal that would frighten felines, prompting them to bolt or retreat. It was imperative that we find a quietish dog with no previous negative experience of cats. I knew any puppies that saw adult dogs growling and barking at cats would invariably copy and learn that behavior, and it was virtually impossible to untrain that response.

So I had to consider the dog's appearance (preferably small, so as not to be overbearing or intimidating); the noise it would make (fairly quiet, with no inclination to bark at animals or people when excited); and its personality (even-keeled, without any aggressive tendencies).

"Well, that's the German shepherds, rottweilers and bloodhounds out of the running, then." Sam smiled as I weighed the various options in the Bramble Hill Farm office one morning. Eventually, I managed to whittle it down to three breeds: the Labrador, the working springer spaniel and the working cocker spaniel. But which one? As Sam did a little drumroll on her desktop, I made my decision.

"It's going to be . . . the working cocker spaniel!"

Working cockers seemed the natural choice, and the more I'd seen them in action, the more convinced I became that they were perfect for the role. They were compact and agile creatures with tons of grit and stamina, epitomized by my favorite police sniffer dog, Rainbow. It happened that my sister, Lynn, and brother Rian had both kept cocker spaniels as pets—albeit those of the "show" variety—and I'd grown incredibly fond of them as a breed. In addition to their good looks, they were incredibly smart, very tactile and excellent problem-solvers.

"And what about gender, Colin?" asked Sam.

"Female, definitely," I responded.

As part of my research, I'd asked dozens of handlers why they'd opted for a male or a female and, generally speaking, it seemed that cocker spaniel females had superior longevity and fewer post-training problems.

So I'd ticked off most things on my detection-dog "wants" list, but another important stipulation remained. Claire, Rob and I had been discussing the qualities of working cocker spaniels—they'd whole-heartedly agreed with my choice of breed, thank goodness—when I decided to drop the bombshell.

"I know this is asking a lot, guys," I said tentatively, "but when we come to source our cat-detection dog, I'd really like her to be a rescue."

My colleagues took a few moments to consider this.

"A rescue dog?" said Rob, raising an eyebrow. "Are you sure that's a good idea?"

"I'm positive it is," I replied. "It's a matter of principle, more than anything, and something I just feel compelled to do. Now let me explain why . . ."

6

A REMARKABLE RESCUE

My devotion to rescue dogs had taken root during my childhood years in Malaysia and Singapore. The streets there were teeming with feral animals, most of whom spent their existence scavenging for food, scrapping with one another or seeking shade in the sweltering heat. My brother David and I were captivated by these scraggly street mutts, and would often smuggle leftover food past my mother for them. We would dash outside to feed these tidbits to the dogs, squealing with delight as they hungrily gorged every last morsel.

Every now and then, however, the dreaded dog van would turn up. Dozens of hounds of all shapes and sizes would be ruthlessly snatched from the street and thrown into the vehicle, never to be seen again. David and I often took matters into our own hands whenever we learned that the "dog killers" were in town. We'd stuff our pockets with pilfered snacks, using them to lure our canine pals away from danger.

"Follow us, you dozy dogs!" we'd yell, darting down narrow alleyways in our shorts and flip-flops, scattering rice balls and bacon rind behind us. I wished I could have rescued every single street stray, but my parents only let David and me keep one dog, an adorable rice-colored mix-breed with wolflike ears. We named her Honey and she became a much-loved family pet.

Back at Medical Detection Dogs' office, I outlined my long-held, deep-rooted principles to Claire and Rob. Every single dog owned by myself or my family had been a rescue, I told them, and I had no plans to deviate from this core value. I also took the opportunity to explain to them that, through my work in the police force and as a pet detective, I'd come across far too many abandoned and neglected dogs. I'd also encountered dozens of wonderful animal shelters and rescue centers who were devoted to adopting out unwanted animals and I was forever committed to their cause.

"I can't really argue with your sentiments," replied Rob. "I'm more than happy to go down the rescue route," he added, "but it might make our search for the right dog a lot longer, and a lot riskier. But, hey, let's give it a go."

Rob contacted his many friends and associates

within the dog world and I put feelers out, too, contacting animal shelters and speaking with former UKPD clients to ask if they knew of any suitable candidates.

The first potential option was Willow, an eleven-month-old working cocker spaniel living in Scotland whose family could no longer look after her. The dog's details were scant but encouraging; by all accounts, she was healthy, friendly and had no discernible issues with cats.

Rob happened to be traveling to Scotland that same week and agreed to visit Willow. Any high hopes I'd had were dashed, however, when he debriefed me over the phone.

"I'm sorry, Colin," he sighed, "but she's not the one you're looking for."

Rob explained that as soon as he'd walked through the front door, poor Willow had run off in the opposite direction and cowered under the kitchen table. Despite his efforts to coax her out, the timid little thing had refused to move a muscle.

"We need the kind of dog that tries to climb on top of a table, Rob, not hide underneath it," I said, sadly crossing Willow off the list.

Our quest continued, but with zero success. Over a period of three months Rob and I assessed half a dozen other rescue spaniels, most of whom showed serious potential on paper but none of whom cut the mustard in reality. Either they were too shy or too snappy or too lazy, or they were too hostile toward cats and other animals.

As time marched on, I began to seriously doubt my own judgment. My precious project—in which I'd invested so much time, thought and effort—seemed to have reached a dead end.

"Going down the rescue-dog route doesn't seem to be working," I moaned to Sarah one evening, having returned home from yet another fruitless dog visit. "To be fair, Rob warned me that it wouldn't be easy. Perhaps it's time for me to get real and broaden my options a bit."

"Maybe you're right," she replied, momentarily looking up from her magazine. "If you're not careful, Colin, you could be waiting forever."

I soon called a meeting with Claire and Rob, at which I suggested—albeit reluctantly—that we should probably extend our search to include reputable breeders. If necessary, the small budget I'd allocated to the project could be used to secure the right dog, even if she wasn't the rescue that I'd pinned my hopes on.

Within a couple of days, Rob had received a tip about Sasha, a beautiful light tan female whose breeder had a surplus of working cocker spaniels. Unlike our previous candidates, she'd sailed through the preliminary assessment, and the next course of action was an intensive, week-long aptitude test. All the signs pointed toward Sasha being our perfect dog, and I was incredibly excited.

I arrived at MDD's headquarters the following Monday—the scheduled start of the trial—only to be greeted at the entrance by an ashen-faced Rob.

"Bad news," he said. "Sasha's not coming."

The breeder had withdrawn her at the eleventh hour, citing a chronic car-sickness problem that she'd "forgotten" to mention. I very much doubted that this was the genuine reason, though; I strongly suspected that the breeder had either gotten a better-priced offer for her dog or had lied to us about Sasha's history and didn't want to be exposed.

We were back to square one, and I felt utterly devastated. I wasn't going to give in, though, and was more determined than ever to succeed. I'd learned to expect holdups and setbacks as par for the course. Experience had taught me that seeing an important mission through to a fruitful outcome was simply an application of effort.

Later that day I went for a long walk around the farm to clear my head and recharge my enthusiasm.

There HAS to be a dog out there, I remember thinking to myself. *It's simply a case of finding her.*

A few weeks later, while I was searching for a missing Labrador, my phone rang. It was Rob, sounding a little more upbeat than he had lately.

"Quick question, Colin . . . you've not totally given up on the rescue-dog idea, have you?"

"No, of course not. That was always Plan A, Rob."

"It's just that I've been online and I've seen a dog that I really like the look of."

An associate of Rob's had alerted him to a black working cocker spaniel female being advertised as a giveaway on a website. Aged around ten months, she'd had three owners in her short life, all of whom had apparently struggled to cope with her unruly and uncontrollable behavior. A stressed-out single mother who had finally reached the end of her rope had posted:

NEEDS A GOOD HOME,

OWNER CANNOT COPE.

"Now, forgive me for sounding negative, Rob, but—"

"Colin, I know exactly what you're going to say. This dog sounds like trouble. But just bear with me on this one. I'm driving up this afternoon to see her, and I'll ring you later."

"What's her name?"

"Molly. Her name's Molly."

Molly. The same name as my friend Anna's dearly departed dog. *That's a good omen*, I thought to myself.

"Right, first the bad news," said Rob, when, as promised, he called me with an update. My shoulders sagged as I braced for yet more disappointment.

"Molly's very, very demanding. She's been badly deprived of love and affection. She suffers from terrible separation anxiety. She barks like crazy when she's frustrated. She steals food from people's plates and treats from their pocket. And she's one of the most willful, wayward and stubborn dogs I've ever met."

"And the good news?" I replied despondently.

"I reckon we've found our dog, Colin."

I rarely found myself lost for words but, on this occasion, I was stunned into silence.

"Yep, you heard me correctly," said Rob, laughing. "Molly's amazing. Sharp as a tack. Bags of energy. Brimming with confidence. She's exactly what we're looking for."

I slowly rubbed my forehead, trying to absorb Rob's good news.

"Don't get me wrong, Colin, she's a dog who'd need an incredible amount of training, but I honestly think she could be perfect for the role."

"This is the best news I've had in ages," I said, allowing myself a little smile.

"But there's one thing I need to run past you," Rob

added, "and it's something I've thought about long and hard. If we do take Molly, I think it's only right that you agree to adopt her once her training's finished, and that would have to be regardless of the outcome, Colin, or her suitability for the role."

"Okay," I said, my mind whirring as I collected my thoughts and processed this unexpected development. It sounded like poor Molly had experienced a wretched start to life, and abandoning her if she failed at training would be pretty heartless. Adopting her "blind" would be a risky decision, considering everything Rob had just said about her—there were certainly no guarantees that we'd be suited to each other—but it was a decision that I was prepared to make. I had spent much of my adulthood offering sanctuary to "problem" pets with troubled pasts. I was quite sure that, with all the love and care that I could muster, I'd be able to give Molly the stable home she craved, regardless of whether or not she became my cat-detection dog. The decision was, as they say, a no-brainer.

"Sure, I'll take her on," I said, visualizing myself and Sarah living in a menagerie of adopted spaniels, none of which had the ability to find lost cats.

Rob secured Molly's ownership, sorted out the paperwork and arranged for her to be transferred to the MDD center. Since my home was two and a half hours away—too distant for a daily commute, particularly with a dog in tow—Molly was to be placed with a local foster family. Because of the MDD center's strict no-kennel policy, all dogs in training were temporarily accommodated in a loving home; this would encourage them to feel as safe and as secure as possible, which would ultimately aid the whole process.

"While we don't know a lot about Molly's history, the fact that she's had numerous owners is bound to have had an impact on her well-being," said Rob, "so it's really important that she feels happy, settled and wanted."

These foster families, I learned, were highly experienced dog caregivers who approached their role with great professionalism. They realized from the outset that the placement was temporary—it could be weeks or months, depending on the duration of the training program—and they closely adhered to the guidance and direction given to them by MDD. While they were expected to offer a high standard of care and attention, the foster families were discouraged from forging close bonds with these working dogs, in view of the fact that they would subsequently be handed over to a permanent owner, or primary handler. I gathered that many of the caregivers were MDD employees who enjoyed the benefits of having a dog in the evenings and weekends while being able to drop them off at the training center during the day.

I would make arrangements for a visit once Molly had settled in at MDD and had ensconced herself with the foster family. In the meantime, Rob emailed me a digital photograph of her that he'd taken during their first encounter. I couldn't help but chuckle at the picture, in which Molly sported a mop of unkempt, shaggy black hair and aimed a moody, defiant stare at the camera lens.

"Have you seen this?" I grinned when I showed Sarah the photo later that evening.

"Bit scruffy, though, isn't she?" she replied, raising her eyebrows.

I immediately set Molly's photo as my phone's screensaver. This dog gave me good vibes and I could hardly wait to meet her.

When I first laid eyes on Molly she was careening around the grounds of Medical Detection Dogs HQ, catching tennis balls that staff members were launching from various directions. The way she sprinted, crouched and leaped to grab those furry lime-green orbs was a joy to behold and, without even knowing this dog, I already felt a distinct sense of pride.

"Just look at her ability to focus, Colin. It's phenomenal," said Rob, who, like me, had been admiring her from afar. "And as for her energy levels . . . well, they're off the scale."

Half an hour later he was ushering me into a nearby building, where I'd finally be meeting Molly face-to-face. Unusual for me, I was beset with nerves, and as the minutes ticked by my head began to pound and my heart began to thump. Molly and I had to feel some kind of connection, otherwise things were in danger of going horribly awry.

Suddenly, the door creaked open and Molly shot into the room, trailed by Rob's colleague Astrid, the specialized trainer who had recently returned from her German police force assignment. I was immediately struck by the dog's bright, sparkly eyes and by the self-assured way she stuck her shiny black nose in the air. She had clearly been groomed since my screensaver photo—her coat was clipped, combed and glossy—and she looked a picture of health and happiness.

"This is one fantastic animal, Colin," remarked Astrid in Spanish-accented English. She explained that she'd spent some time with Molly, performing a few simple exercises in the training lab, and had already become smitten.

"Do let me know if you ever change your mind about adopting her," she winked, "because I'd gladly take her off your hands."

Molly then began to scoot around the room, sniffing each dusty corner, sussing out every inch of space, sizing up every human. When she finally caught sight of me, perched tentatively on an office chair, she paused for a moment and tilted her head curiously.

Who are you, mister? she seemed to be saying. *Why are you here? What exactly are you going to bring to my world, huh?*

"Hey, just look at that, Colin." Rob smiled. "I do believe Molly's weighing you up."

I purposely didn't call her across or crouch down to say hello. I knew how perceptive dogs could be about human behavior and I didn't want to transfer any feelings of unease. Instead, I just stayed put and held her gaze, while thoughts swirled around my head.

Well, well, young lady, I mused. *What are you thinking? Do you think we can work together? Are you ready for a fabulous journey?* Rob and Astrid were highly amused at this mutual sizing up.

"I'm not sure which one of you is going to make the first move here," chortled Astrid.

As it happened, it was Molly who broke the stalemate. She slowly sidled over to me, gently nudged the side of my thigh with her snout and, much to my amazement, deftly sprang into my lap.

Yeah, I think I like the look of this fella seemed to be

the gist of it. She shuffled her bottom into a more comfortable position. *I can work with this guy* . . .

I nuzzled in close, ruffled her neck and looked across at Rob and Astrid, who were beaming like a pair of proud parents.

"I think Molly's made up her mind," I said, smiling, as she moved around to face the two of them. "And I reckon I have, too."

I finally had my dog—I just knew she was The One—and the feeling of relief was intense. It had been a long, hard slog to get this far, and it had left me feeling emotionally exhausted. During the previous two years barely a day had passed that I hadn't thought about my project, and my obsession had exacted a heavy toll on my business and on my home life. Some of my private-eye clients had closed their accounts, complaining that they'd been unable to get hold of me. Also, there'd been countless weekends when Sarah had been left home alone while I'd met with various canine experts. To her credit, Sarah had been incredibly supportive, patiently listening to all my gripes and grumbles.

The day I met Molly, however, I returned home brimming with glee.

"You'll never guess what, Sarah, but I've found my dog," I grinned, hugging her close and planting a big kiss on her cheek. "The search is finally over. Molly's absolutely amazing and, all being well, one day she'll be here with us . . ."

"That's great. I'm so pleased," my partner replied, not entirely convincingly.

That night, I made a point of phoning Anna. She had been closely following my progress and knew all about the trials and tribulations I'd faced. I also felt that I owed my friend a great deal, since she had introduced me to Claire and Rob in the first place.

"You won't believe it, Anna," I said. "Molly is just perfect. Beyond my wildest dreams, in fact."

"I'm so thrilled for you, Colin," she replied. "And I know MDD will do a marvelous job with her. There's no way they'd agree to train Molly if they didn't think she was the right dog."

For the next half an hour we chatted all things Molly, focusing particularly on her health and well-being. Anna's expertise in this regard was second to none, and she offered me so much invaluable advice and guidance, regarding the right nutrition for working dogs, for example, and dealing with canine separation anxiety. By the time I'd hung up I'd collected a long list of the things that I needed to consider and all the topics I needed to familiarize myself with.

At last, I thought, leaning back in my office chair. *We're finally getting somewhere . . .*

For the duration of her training—the expected time-scale was six months—Molly would remain at MDD and continue living with her foster family in the evenings and on weekends. Under the expert guidance of Rob and Astrid, she would be taught how to scent-match through exposure to a host of different odors and would learn how to discriminate between them. As for me, I was allowed to visit Molly regularly to observe her in action, after which Rob would give me a prog-ress report. I would also get the chance to spend some quality time with her—lots of walks, chats and tennis-ball action—in order to get to know my dog better.

Molly performed brilliantly at MDD and adapted beautifully to her training program, yet within a few months she began to develop some worrying behav-ioral issues away from the HQ. Since her arrival, Molly had become very close to Astrid (perhaps too close, I'd noted) and she had suffered severe separation anxi-ety when Astrid had left MDD to pursue other projects. While the MDD experts were able to manage Molly's fretfulness at the center, her foster family faced enor-mous problems at home. Being a very willful dog, she'd started to bend rules and take liberties—jumping on the

*The brilliant Mark Doggett with the first cat
that Molly found during training at MDD*

sofa, stealing food off tables and ignoring commands—
and was effectively displaying the same disobedience
that had driven her previous owner to give her away.
This regression, we all realized, needed to be curbed
before it jeopardized the whole project.

"There's no way a badly behaved, ill-disciplined
Molly will be able to work in the field," I said to Rob.
"This needs to be nipped in the bud."

A canine behavioral expert who worked for MDD—
the aptly named Mark Doggett—was drafted to correct
Molly's conduct and, in order to restore some balance
to her life, she was transferred from the foster home to
Mark's full-time care. She would reside in his house with
his two pet dogs, where she'd be taught to adapt her
behavior and to adhere to strict boundaries, far away from

any distractions. As for her scent-match training, Mark—under the guidance of MDD—would continue this regimen away from the center, essentially building upon the excellent foundations already laid by Rob and Astrid.

This intensive one-to-one therapy would last for at least three months, which meant that the final handover—when Molly was due to join me permanently—would have to be postponed.

While I was deeply disappointed, I agreed that it was the correct thing to do and was prepared to remain patient. I'd waited so long for this project to materialize and I was in no rush to get it wrong.

Molly's transfer to another caregiver was far from ideal, but when I watched Mark interacting with her for the first time I was convinced that she was in safe hands. Not only did he have a brilliant understanding of Molly, he also had a calming effect upon her and I could see exactly why MDD had decided to assign him to this role.

Mark encouraged me to pay regular visits to his home (I'd often drop by after a progress meeting with Claire and Rob) and he was more than happy for me to take Molly off for a long walk, just the two of us, man and dog. I savored every moment we spent together, and found each goodbye incredibly difficult.

Initially, Mark's progress with Molly seemed slow-going and his weekly reports appeared to identify a litany of problems.

"What I'm trying to do is pinpoint the issues that are stimulating Molly's disobedience so that I can address her negative behavior," he told me during one phone conversation, explaining that he was employing a rewards-based system in order to encourage her to act in a positive manner. For instance, during play sessions with Mark's pet dogs, Molly would be ordered to wait her turn, something that she found very difficult. However, if she did as she was told and curbed her friskiness and impatience, she'd be rewarded with some tennis ball–related fun and games.

Indoor rules and regulations were paramount, too, in order to restore some decorum and discipline to her behavior. She wasn't allowed in the master bedroom or upstairs, for example, or in the kitchen when food was being eaten or prepared.

Fortunately, by month two, Mark confirmed that my little cocker spaniel was finally making fantastic headway; she was responding well to her behavioral training, and—much to my relief—was continuing to achieve excellent results with her scent-matching sessions.

This breakthrough meant that we could set a date for the big handover: Friday, 23 December 2016. However, before I could bring Molly home for good, we were both required to undergo two weeks of intensive training together at MDD. It was literally a pass-or-fail period, certainly not a case of "Now you're trained, off you go . . ." Unless Molly and I could prove that we could work as an effective unit, the MDD seal of approval wouldn't be bestowed on us and, as a result, my project would be in jeopardy.

During this crucial two-week period we spent a great deal of time in various locations near the training center, starting at nine o'clock prompt every morning. Mark or Rob carefully demonstrated Molly's intricate odor-detecting techniques and, in addition, taught me how to set up simulated searches by concealing different scent samples in a variety of outdoor environments. Each task became progressively more complex; early in the two-week session we'd asked Molly to detect a single scent sample in a small garden, for example, but toward the end we'd hidden the target scent in a large farmyard, together with two contrasting samples that Molly had to disregard. She completed every task with ease and, as she heeded my commands with confidence, I felt my own confidence levels soaring. It wasn't just Molly that was being tested, after all; I was being constantly watched and assessed.

"Where did you think you went wrong that time, Colin?" Mark would ask, peering over my shoulder. It was all incredibly intense.

Following each training session—and while Molly enjoyed a well-deserved breather—I'd sit down with

Rob or Mark to go through some theory. They would share their expertise and bolster my knowledge, explaining how scent profiles could be impacted by meteorology and topography, for example, or outlining the intricacies of a working cocker spaniel's olfactory system. We covered a wide range of topics, including the correct use of voice tone during searches, the application of certain types of play and the benefits of implementing a rewards system.

As the two weeks progressed, and as Molly began to realize that this Colin fella was going to play a significant role in her life, my detection-dog-in-waiting and I became even closer. The MDD team were extremely heartened by the deep bond we'd forged— our mutual affection was there for all to see—and they were delighted to witness us working in harmony. It felt like Molly and I had been buddied up like a traditional detective duo, and everyone was thrilled to see my sidekick and me hitting it off so well.

"Your teamwork is outstanding, Colin," said Mark as we drove to a nearby wood one morning for yet another practice session, while Molly sat in her dog crate, champing at the bit. "Having that deep understanding of each other was always going to be key, but from what I can see, you've both cracked it."

At the end of each training day Molly and I would travel to my parents' home, which was only a forty minutes' drive from the center. They had agreed to let me stay with them during the two weeks—from Monday to Friday—and were particularly glad to meet the latest addition to the Butcher household. *Wow, this is exciting!* Molly seemed to say as we drove away from MDD after our first full day together.

Where are we going? Who are we meeting?

As I'd expected, Molly turned on the charm with my parents, but they knew a challenging dog when they saw one.

"Goodness, she's got plenty of energy, hasn't she?" remarked my mother, with admirable understatement, while Molly bounced off the kitchen cupboards and surfaces in hot pursuit of a brand-new tennis ball. "Does Sarah know what she's let herself in for?"

"Sure," I said, smiling nervously.

By the end of the first week, my parents were exhausted—Molly had struggled with the change of environment and had proved to be rather high-maintenance—and their kitchen floor was carpeted with black dog hair. Being devoted animal-lovers themselves, however, they didn't care one bit.

Halfway through our training period, on a bitterly cold Friday evening, I brought Molly home for the first time. Prior to her arrival, I'd made a number of essential adaptations in the house in order to make it as dog-friendly as possible. I converted our downstairs utility room into Molly's own little den, a place where she could retreat for some peace, quiet and solitude. Then, despite Sarah's resistance ("Surely it only needs one place to sleep, Colin?"), I placed a selection of deluxe dog beds in the warmest parts of the house. I also ordered plenty of Molly's favorite foods (including treats of raw black pudding, raw beef jerky, hot-dog sausages and cheddar cheese) and, after a visit to my local pet store, I upped my supply of dog toys and playthings.

Anxious to devote as much time as possible to Molly while she settled in, I'd carefully adjusted my work routine, too, canceling all appointments or investigations that required me to be away from home for more than a few hours. Also, I chose not to book any major vacations for a period of six months, since I didn't want to be parted from Molly at this vital stage in her life. That wasn't exactly welcome news to Sarah, who, for the previous four years, had spent most of February relaxing by my side at our friend's Caribbean villa.

Suffice to say that my girlfriend wasn't overly impressed when she arrived home from work that Friday night in December. Molly and I had spent the whole day conducting training searches in the countryside, wading through streams and crawling under hedges, and had both ended up decidedly wet and smelly. I was in the process of cramming the damp contents of my workbag into the washing machine when I heard Sarah's key turning in the lock and her stilettos *tip-tap*ping down the hallway.

"Oh my god, this place reeks!" she exclaimed, standing in the kitchen doorway, looking pristine in a navy-blue business suit and cream blouse.

"Hi, sweetheart." I grinned and gestured toward a mud-spattered Molly, who was spread-eagle across my raincoat. "Look who's here!"

I walked over to peck my girlfriend's cheek, only for her to recoil in horror.

"Look at the state of you both!" she shrieked. "You're absolutely covered in muck. And please . . . what the *heck* is that smell?"

"It's just wet dog, darling. It'll vanish once Molly dries out, I promise."

"That thing needs a bloody bath. It stinks," she said, glaring at Molly, and then at me. "And so do you."

She placed her leather bag on a kitchen chair before turning around to hang up her jacket. Quick as a flash, my mischievous mutt stuffed her wet snout into the bag and proceeded to rummage around, dragging out a purse and a packet of tissues, which she began to shred gleefully.

"I thought you said this dog was trained?" yelled my horrified girlfriend, swiping her bag off the chair.

"She's just a bit inquisitive, that's all," I answered meekly as Sarah flounced out of the kitchen, slamming the door behind her.

Molly cocked her head to one side before blinking at me with woeful eyes.

What did I do wrong? Why doesn't that lady like me?

"Don't you worry, Molls," I whispered, retrieving the drool-soaked tissues. "This is all new to Sarah. It's nothing personal. She just needs a bit of time to get used to you. But here's one piece of advice: steer clear of ladies' handbags, eh?"

I patted her head affectionately and she snuffled my palm in return.

"Anyway, missy, let's get you in the bath," I said. "Sarah's right. You do stink."

- - ~ -

I hardly got any rest that night. Molly whined constantly whenever I tried to pad back to my bedroom for some sleep, and she seemed very tense and anxious. The MDD team had already briefed me on what to expect, advising me to give my dog plenty of love—and lots of latitude—as she slowly grew accustomed to her new environment.

"Allow her to bond to you, Colin, because she's desperate to do so," said Rob. "Do whatever it takes to make her feel safe and secure."

I ended up dragging a duvet to Molly's den so that I could stay with her throughout the night. I lay quietly beside her bed, calming and comforting her until she curled herself up and closed her eyes.

The following week I was finally allowed to bring Molly home on a permanent basis. She and I had passed our two-week test with flying colors—at times it had felt as rigorous as my Royal Navy air-crew training—and she was good and ready to be transferred to my care. We bid a fond farewell to all the staff, who showered Molly with treats. My dog stuck to my heel the whole time, like a clingy toddler.

I'm not leaving your side, Dad, she seemed to be implying. *I'm going nowhere . . .*

We then made a detour to Claire's office. She had, of course, played an integral role from start to finish, enabling the whole project to take place at her busy center and allowing me to work with her incredible in-house team. She had been instrumental in connecting me with Astrid, too; this pioneering scent-matching expert had been absolutely pivotal to Molly's unique training program, painstakingly applying the same scientific techniques to a working cocker spaniel that she'd used with the German police force's sniffer dogs.

"It's been a total privilege to play my part, Colin,"

beamed Claire, "and suffice to say, you've got an extraordinarily special dog on your hands."

As she said this, Molly held out her paw for Claire to shake, and I'm pretty sure I noticed my colleague blink away a tear.

"Goodbye, Molly." She smiled as we exited her office. "I wish you all the luck in the world."

Back outside, I spotted Rob and Mark chatting beside the huge training field which, over the past nine months, had become Molly's favorite playground. They both waved when they saw us ambling over and laughed as they watched Molly vanish under a nearby hedge, reappearing with a moldy old tennis ball between her teeth.

"You guys have been fantastic," I said, embracing them both. "You've gone above and beyond, you really have, and there's no way I could have done this without you."

Their combined knowledge and experience had propelled this project forward, and I would be forever in their debt.

"You've got yourself an exceptional dog there," replied Mark, crouching down low to give Molly a heartfelt hug. "She's one in a million."

"Thanks for believing in us, Colin," added Rob. "It's been a pleasure working with you both."

A few minutes later I was driving out of the parking

lot and, as I said goodbye to this fantastic center of excellence, I found my mind casting back to the events of the previous spring. Molly and I had arrived here separately, unsure where the future was going to take us, and now we were leaving as a team, beginning an amazing adventure together.

✦ ✦ ✦

My car phone buzzed with well-wishers during the journey home. So many friends and relatives had been following Molly's progress and they were all thrilled to learn that she'd graduated with honors and was coming home.

Sarah called to finalize arrangements for our Christmas break. We had made plans to join my parents and siblings (and their assorted spaniels) at a wonderful dog-friendly hotel in the country.

"I've started to gather Molly's things together in the hallway," she said, "but if you think we're traveling in my car with all that dog hair, you're very much mistaken."

Using my dog's name instead of "it" was a promising development, I decided, but I was under no illusions: Sarah still needed a lot of winning over.

As the skies began to darken, I hit some holiday traffic and the car came to a standstill. With no imminent sign of movement, I turned off the engine, peered into my rearview mirror and began to talk to Molly. I chatted to her for a good twenty minutes as she stared at me through the back panel of her travel crate, her tail occasionally whacking against the sides.

I told her how much she was going to enjoy Christmas, and how the whole Butcher family was so looking forward to meeting her. I told her that, once New Year was upon us, I'd be taking her over to Pet Detectives HQ—to the lovely Bramble Hill Farm—where she'd be able to play in the meadows, frolic through the woods and practice lots and lots of searches. And while we waited for the traffic to subside, I told her about some of the dogs I'd known and loved in my life.

"But now I've got you." I smiled, gazing at Molly's reflection in the mirror as she attentively cocked her head to one side. "You've worked so hard, my gorgeous girl, and you've made me so very, very proud. And just think . . . in a few weeks' time we might have found our first missing cat. How amazing would that be?"

Boof-boof-boof-boof went her tail against her crate, like some sort of doggy Morse code.

A few moments later the cars began moving and our journey south continued. Molly and I were homeward bound.

SKILLS AND DRILLS AT
BRAMBLE HILL

Having Molly home for good was the best feeling in the world. We had had an idyllic Christmas—my dog had been loved and fussed over by staff, guests and the entire Butcher family and had coped remarkably well with the attention—but it was with a certain sense of relief that, on New Year's Day, I unlatched my front door at home. With the festivities nearly over, it was time to devote some serious one-to-one attention to my new little housemate.

"Home, sweet home, Molls," I said as she loped off down the hallway, snuffling the skirting boards.

"Don't let her mark the walls, Colin," said Sarah coolly, before heading to the bedroom to unpack her suitcase. "Oh, and her feet need wiping."

"Molly has paws, honey, not feet," I replied.

"Well, whatever they are, they need cleaning or else she'll dirty the carpet."

I glanced at my forlorn-looking dog, who had clearly sensed Sarah's dislike.

I wiped my paws on the way in, Dad . . . she seemed to be saying. *I am trying, I promise* . . .

Also accompanying us that day was my twenty-year-old son, Sam, who'd opted to spend the final week of his vacation with me before heading back to Manchester University. He had first met Molly at Medical Detection Dogs the previous autumn—it had been love at first sight—and he was more than willing to stick around to help her settle in. December had been a disruptive month for my little cocker spaniel (she'd stayed in many different places and had met countless new faces) and it was time for her to obtain some much-needed stability.

Sarah returned to work—she was visibly relieved to escape the Molly-related mayhem—and Sam and I stayed at home to help our dog adjust. My son was an absolute godsend, as it happened, and spent much of the week chatting to Molly in the kitchen or playing catch in the garden, alleviating her angst and helping to make her feel as safe and secure as possible. He and I had been devoted to our pets down the years—"Care first for those who can't care for themselves" had been a long-standing fatherly mantra of mine—and I was so pleased to see that my love of animals had rubbed off on him, too.

Molly was loath to leave my side in those first few

days, which, considering the upheaval she'd suffered, was hardly unexpected. For a rescue dog who'd had a string of owners—followed by a long spell at MDD—separation anxiety was the likeliest of consequences. Her insecurity showed up in different ways, I discovered. When I greeted her in the morning she'd respond by nibbling the inside of my palm, like a puppy nursing her mother, which was her way of keeping me close and reinforcing our bond. By allowing her to do this, I was effectively letting her know that I'd always be there for her and, unlike her previous owners, would never abandon her.

I found that she constantly followed me around the house, too, nervously jumping up whenever I tried to leave a room and, moments later, suddenly appearing at my heel. All I could do at this stage was try and pacify her. I would crouch down low, avoiding any unexpected movements, and would stroke rather than hug her (like many dogs, she didn't like the feeling of being smothered).

"Molly, sweetheart, I'm just going to the hallway to pick up some mail," I'd say quietly. "I'll be back in two shakes of your tail, I promise."

She would invariably pad after me, though, her expression lovelorn, and for the first two weeks I just went with the flow and let her follow me around. Thereafter, however, I spent a lot of time training Molly to understand that my exiting a room wasn't a negative act. If I planned to pop out of my home office to make coffee, for example—and Molly was lying yards away in her bed—I'd quietly attract her attention, telling her to "stay" and rewarding her with a couple of small treats before I slowly opened the door. Within a few days her stalking behavior improved. She soon realized that I wasn't leaving her forever and that she could count on my return. To help her feel close to me at all times, I draped each of her beds with one of my fleeces or sweatshirts, too, confident that my unique scent "signature" would create a sense of comfort.

Fundamentally, our future success as a partnership—either as pet and owner, or as fellow sleuths—would rely on Molly investing her trust in me and understanding that I wasn't going to let her down. I didn't know much about Molly's history, but I knew enough about dogs to realize that she still felt vulnerable and that she was emotionally scarred by some bad memories. If I noticed her flinching at a sudden movement in the kitchen, for instance, or shuddering as the garage door slammed shut, I'd get in close and offer her reassurance. I could only assume that someone had once lashed out at her or had locked her away in a shed.

"It's okay," I'd whisper softly, gently cradling her head in my palms. "You're safe with me, Molly, and I'll always be here for you. Always."

Having had previous experience with rescue animals,

I knew that, while dogs tended to live "in the moment," in some cases it could take a long time for a mistreated animal to erase painful experiences. The best way to manage that situation was, I'd found, to provide my dogs with unlimited, unconditional love and affection, layering on those good memories in order to stifle the bad.

I also introduced regular indoor play sessions to keep her occupied, heeding Mark's advice to split her toys into two boxes. Box One contained Molly's comfort toys, which she was allowed to keep by her bed and which she could play with at all times (she became particularly fond of a squeaky rat, which she'd drag around the house). Box Two contained Colin's toys, however, and was kept on top of the fridge, well out of Molly's reach. These playthings could only be used on my terms and my dog was under strict instructions not to keep them, run away with them or rough them up. She would often sit in the kitchen and whine plaintively in their direction, but I had to stand firm.

"It's about instilling discipline," I remember Mark telling me. "Molly's a very headstrong dog and she's got to understand what's off-limits."

~ ~ ~ ~ ~

While she'd been at MDD, Mark had taught Molly a long list of unique dog commands—some for day-to-day usage, some work-related—that my son, Sam, and

I were obliged to learn and use. Mark had really cus-
tomized a whole new language for her, in an attempt to
address the disobedience that she'd shown at her foster family's home. There, she'd blatantly ignored standard instructions like "Sit" and "Down"—she'd willfully
done the opposite—and had also developed a worrying aversion to the word "No." The problem had no
doubt come from her caregivers' unreliable discipline
techniques, coupled with the fact that this sneaky little
pooch had learned how to get her way.

Her caregivers had admonished her with a sharp
"No" whenever she'd jumped up to pinch food off a
plate, for instance, but after five minutes' worth of pawing and whining they'd given in and offered up the bis-
cuit as a treat. Naturally, Molly soon began to associate
this purportedly negative command with a positive
outcome; to her, "No" essentially meant "Yes."

Prior to the big handover, therefore, Mark had
decided to reconfigure Molly's entire command system
by embedding a brand-new set of words and erasing a
legion of others. So "No" was replaced with "Ah-ah";
"Sit" became "Stay"; "Hup" denoted "Jump up here";
and "Off" meant all four paws on the ground. He'd also
tailored some working commands, too, designed to be
used during field drills and real-life searches.

Sam and I spent hours practicing these new words
and phrases with Molly.

"Ah-ah," I'd say, wagging my finger as she jumped onto a chair, and she would meekly sit back down when she realized I meant business.

I was frequently on the phone with Mark in those early days, since I was eager to understand Molly's various habits and behaviors. This included a trait she'd developed indoors, shortly after Sam had returned to school. Most evenings would find Sarah and me in the living room, either reading, watching a movie or catching up with emails. Once we'd settled ourselves onto the sofa, though, Molly would detect that the focus had shifted away from her. Annoyed, she took to repetitively pacing around the house, embarking upon a two-minute circuit that took her around the back of the sofa, along the living room wall, around the dining-room table, past the large bookcase, in front of the TV, along the fireplace, behind Sarah's chair and then finally back to me again.

Molly would perform about twenty laps until she became so worn out she would flop into her bed. Once she regained her breath, however, she'd start the circuit all over again and, despite my efforts, couldn't be calmed or distracted.

"How am I supposed to concentrate on this film?" griped Sarah one Saturday evening as a panting Molly obstructed the TV screen for the fifteenth time. "It's driving me insane, Colin. Can't you do something about it?"

My suggestion to mount the television on the wall was met with an icy stare.

"Okay," I said meekly. "I get the message. Leave it with me."

The following Monday I called the Mark Doggett hotline. "Molly's definitely attention-seeking—and she may well be missing Sam, too—but there are ways you can break this Grand Prix circuit," said my canine-behavior mentor, before outlining a strict plan of action.

For the next few nights, instead of sitting on the sofa, I'd sit reading my book with my back against the living room radiator or against the dining-room wall. My outstretched legs presented her with a physical obstacle that interrupted her flow, threw her off-kilter and allowed me to divert her attention with a toy for a couple of minutes. Mark's advice to hide her favorite beef-jerky snacks along her "course" to break her repetitive behavior worked, too. She would soon become distracted by the scent, try to locate the snack and, when she succeeded, she'd receive some serious praise from yours truly. Soon enough, the intensity of the circuits slowed down and they eventually came to a halt.

"Thank heavens for that," sighed Sarah with some relief one night, having finally watched an entire movie, uninterrupted, for the first time in weeks.

If I was going to keep a strong-willed dog like Molly in check, I needed to establish some rigid house rules. I knew I'd only be asking for trouble if I didn't lay down the law.

After much contemplation, and after consulting with Mark, I decided to give her freedom to move around most of the house, with a couple of no-go areas. She wasn't allowed to enter either of our two bathrooms—unless I was giving her a post-walk bath—and she was also forbidden from entering the master and the guest bedroom. I spent hours training her to recognize these particular boundaries, and even made them more conspicuous by covering the metal carpet thresholds with two widths of silver-gray duct tape.

"Ah-ah, Moll-yyyy . . . ," I'd say if she ever attempted to trespass. *"Ah-aaaah."*

Molly being Molly, though, she would constantly—and quite literally—try to cross the line. Sometimes I'd spot her lolling in the hallway on the correct side of the tape, a few feet away from our bedroom. Then, when she thought I wasn't looking, she'd slowly outstretch her paw so that it touched the tape and, bit by bit, shuffle her body forward.

"Moll-yyyyy," I'd scold, and she'd retract her paw immediately, like it was attached to a spring. Then, moments later, out of the corner of my eye, I'd spy her long black snout edging toward the threshold.

"MOLL-YYYY . . ."

It was a constant battle of wills between Molly and me, and sometimes it took a gargantuan effort to maintain the upper hand. Watching her forever testing these boundaries was highly entertaining. She was determined, but I knew that if I was going to keep her safe during live searches, she'd have to obey and understand my commands. "No" meant "No" (or, in Molly's case, "Ah-ah" meant "Ah-ah").

Jumping onto our comfy leather sofa was also off-limits, but that didn't stop Molly trying to push her luck. Sometimes she'd take advantage of dark, wintry nights, especially if my reading lamp was the sole light source, to stealthily creep up onto the settee, unnoticed. Five minutes later I'd glance to my left, only to catch sight of a pair of beady eyes glinting beside me.

"Oi, off you get, you cheeky minx!" I'd say, laughing and giving her a gentle nudge.

She was a smart little cookie and a master problem-solver, and her sneakiness knew no bounds.

I was particularly strict about my dog's domestic eating habits. Following her evening meal, Molly would be walked for half an hour and then, while Sarah or myself prepared our own dinner, she'd be settled into her living room bed. In common with every dog I've owned, I never, ever let her watch me eat and refused to feed her any leftovers from my plate.

Hoping to stay on Sarah's good side, I did all I could to keep Molly in check at home.

"Molly's been nice and quiet, hasn't she?" said Sarah, after I'd prepared a nice, romantic three-course meal, while my fed-and-walked dog snoozed contentedly in her bed. I was pretty sure I detected a hint—just a smidgeon—of affection.

There was no denying that Molly's first few weeks at home were challenging. No sooner had I eliminated one behavioral trait than another would appear—it was like a merry-go-round of dog problems—and I was regularly on the phone with poor Mark, or my pal Anna, asking for advice and guidance.

Soon we were faced with another hurdle to overcome. Molly had limited experience in urban areas—she'd spent much of her early life cooped up in kitchens and garages, I suspected, before being transferred to the rural MDD center. She needed to get used to busy public places. Aware that this wasn't going to be straightforward, I approached things step by step, first taking Molly for short walks in Cranleigh High Street, then building up to longer trips into the town center. I researched all the dog-friendly venues in the area, gradually exposing her to a variety of shops and restaurants that could assure us of a pleasant welcome.

Initially, Molly was totally overstimulated by all these fresh sights, sounds and smells and would bounce around like a hyperactive, sugar-fueled toddler. She would create havoc in any eateries we visited, making a mad dash to greet every customer who walked through the door, wrapping her lead around my calf as she did so and almost cutting off my blood supply. Sometimes she'd refuse to enter certain premises, and on other occasions she'd stick to my side like glue, often panicking if she lost sight of me. I raised my concerns with Mark, and we concluded that one of Molly's changes of ownership had probably taken place in a café. She might have arrived with one owner and left with another. I was determined to help her overcome her anxiety. I needed her to understand that, although there'd be occasions when I'd have to leave her alone, she could always guarantee my return.

Mark and I devised a strategy to expose her to as many cafés as possible, and to apply some relaxation techniques once she got there. During the first few visits Molly watched me like a hawk, tracking my every move. She gradually began to unwind, however, and it wasn't long before she could last a full minute without checking on my whereabouts.

Some trips out were more successful than others, though. One Sunday afternoon Sarah and I decided to brave a café with Molly in tow. While we both had a bite to eat, Molly sat obediently under the table, her lead coiled securely around Sarah's chair leg. As we dove into our desserts—sorbet for me, cheesecake for Sarah—some other diners, accompanied by a large, handsome Irish setter, took a table across the open-plan eating area. Unbeknownst to us, they'd come armed with an egg-shaped, treat-filled plastic toy to keep their pooch occupied.

Then, just as Sarah got up to go to the restroom, I answered an important phone call from a client. Realizing that I was distracted, Molly took the opportunity to careen across the pub in a bid to grab the amazing dog toy she'd spied from afar. Sarah's chair was still attached, its legs scraping loudly behind her. The darkness of Molly's coat—together with the place's dim lighting—made it look like a ghostly chair was flying across the room.

"Andy, I'll call you back," I whispered to my client.

With her prey clamped firmly in her jaw, Molly charged back—upending some drinks as she did so— and dropped the toy at my feet, which won her a few loud guffaws from fellow patrons. The landlord wasn't impressed, however, emerging moments later with a mop and bucket while muttering about irresponsible owners and their uncontrollable dogs.

"Bad girl, Molly," I admonished, blushing from head to toe, before returning the toy to a rather startled-looking Irish setter.

On a fresh and frosty afternoon, Molly enjoyed her very first visit to Bramble Hill Farm.

"Something tells me you're going to love it here, Molly," I said, holding her gaze in my rearview mirror as we neared the farmhouse. As soon as I released her from her dog crate she tore across the driveway, scattering gravel as she went, before hurtling into the large meadow facing the farmhouse. She zoomed around its perimeter in a joyful gallop, springing over frozen puddles, gulping down the chilly air and disturbing a pair of hooded crows, who cawed their displeasure at the unwanted intrusion. I watched from the stone patio and smiled contentedly to myself. Over the coming months, Molly and I were destined to spend hours and hours at Bramble Hill, yet she already looked like she belonged there.

On the command of "Molly, come," she scampered back with a *Wow, Dad, this is FUN!* look on her face, whereupon I rehooked her leash and attached her training harness.

"Let's go and explore," I said, flicking the ice crystals off her paws and wiping the water droplets from her whiskers, then leading her farther down into this 500-acre estate. I was excited to familiarize my dog with all the various wildlife scents (she needed to be able to distinguish them from cat odors during searches), so our first stop was a field known as Fox Cover, so called because—in the warmer months—it housed a fox's den. Molly had a good old sniff around, poking her snout into the broad hole and doubtless picking up the faint scent of the previous season's fox cubs, as well as that of the small mammals they'd feasted on. We then sauntered over to a labyrinth of rabbit warrens—which Molly studied and snuffled with interest—before heading over to a dense area of woodland, our arrival sending pheasants and woodcocks off to fly toward a thicket of silver birch.

As the sun began to set, I guided Molly toward my favorite place in Bramble Hill Farm. Shepherd's Rest was a small ridge located at the dead center of the estate and was easily identifiable by the presence of two ancient, majestic oak trees that had loomed large in the area for centuries. With its calm and peaceful setting and its panoramic views, it had become my little haven, the place I visited to clear my head.

I perched on a large, flat tree root and rested my back against the trunk. A tired-looking Molly plodded over and plonked herself down, leaning into me for comfort as the winter breeze began to sharpen. We sat quietly for a good ten minutes, until a flurry of activity caused Molly to spring to her feet. I felt her muscles flinch and her heartbeat quicken as a trio of roe deer broke cover from the woodland and crossed a footpath before grazing on the lush wet grass.

I put a comforting arm around Molly's warm little body, drew her close and saw two friendly brown eyes gazing up at me.

"Isn't this lovely, Molls?" I said as a wave of emotion washed over me. Here I was, in my favorite spot, with my yearned-for dog, and—at that precise moment—without a care in the world. True, there had been days when Molly had been extremely challenging. Since moving in she'd destroyed a variety of clothing and furnishings and had caused a few accidents around the house, albeit nothing that couldn't be cleaned or replaced. Overall, however, she'd made excellent progress with her scent-match training and the good days had far outweighed the bad.

While Molly and I still had a long way to go before we could truly call ourselves a team, the future was looking very promising, and things could only get better. All things considered, having Molly in my life was wonderful.

Molly's second phase of field training, this time with me as her handler, began in earnest in mid-January 2017. If my dog and I were going to find some missing cats—and offer genuine hope to their distressed owners—I needed to be absolutely certain that Molly was on top of her game before she was deployed. I spent hours in the office devising a varied program of tests, skills exercises and mock searches, many of which had been drilled into us by Mark and Astrid at MDD.

"You need to be so inventive and imaginative with these searches, Colin," Mark had said at the time, "and you must never forget how smart she is."

He went on to explain that, in order to find the sample, Molly would do her utmost to track my scent. To combat this—she wouldn't be able to rely on my scent when she was tracking an actual missing pet—I'd either have to walk around in different directions while I planted the sample or ask someone else to do the deed instead. Before we could start these practice searches, however, I had to obtain some genuine cat-hair samples. Initially, I'd asked some feline-owning friends and neighbors to oblige, but knocking on doors to obtain fur clumps from cat beds soon became quite time-consuming.

It was Sam who decided to call a rescue center in South London. Not only did they have a plethora of cats of varying breeds—and we needed samples from as wide a variety as possible—they seemed more than willing to grant my rather unusual request.

"Happy to help, Colin," the manager said, smiling, when Molly and I arrived at the bustling center one morning. The staff couldn't believe how feline-friendly Molly was, noting that they'd never met a dog that had no inclination to bark at cats, or to chase them. They were also intrigued about the cat-detection project—most particularly the scent-recognition process—but were equally impressed with our ultimate goal.

"If Molly's going to be finding lost cats, that'll mean fewer of them will end up here, in all sorts of distress," said the manager. He explained that some of their cats had been brought to them from outside the London area and, since they hadn't been microchipped, it was unlikely they'd ever be reunited with their owners.

Molly and I waited patiently in the reception area as the staff—wearing sterile gloves so as to avoid cross-contamination—visited some resident cats to collect the samples, gently rubbing pieces of cloth around the cats' faces in order to gather as much hair and scent as possible. Plastic bags were sealed and marked: Bag A was the "target" sample, which I would split into two parts, one part to hide and the other to present to Molly as the source sample. Bag B was the "environmental" sample that would enable Molly to discriminate the missing cat's scent from the background scents associated with the cat's home.

"I can't tell you how much I appreciate this," I said, when the manager emerged carrying a shoebox stacked with plastic bags. I popped a generous donation in their collection box and purchased half a dozen secondhand cat carriers. It was the very least I could do for this army of animal aficionados.

Back at Bramble Hill Farm, winter gradually yielded to spring. The frosted ground began to soften underfoot, the bare branches started to bud and the clearings became a white-yellow sea of snowdrops and crocuses. The farm contained plenty of nooks and crannies—from rotting logs and stone walls to unused hay barns and derelict stables—and the following morning I asked Sam to hide a target sample somewhere within the sprawling estate. It was what I called a "blind search," meaning that Molly and I had no idea where the sample was hidden and would have to work closely as a team to find it.

Then it was time to introduce Molly to the matching "A" sample, which had been transferred to a sterilized jam jar, in order for her to perform the scent match. I released her from her crate, controlling my body language, lowering the tone of my voice and carefully choosing my words so as to communicate that it was now time for work, not play. I attached my dog's work "uniform"—a bright yellow reflective harness—slipped her black-pudding treats into my utility belt, then crouched down low beside her.

Carefully unscrewing the jam jar, I issued the unique command that Mark and Astrid had taught me at Medical Detection Dogs.

"Toma," I said, which was the signal for Molly to inhale the cat scent. She poked her nose into the sample jar, sniffing and snuffling for a few seconds in order to invite the aroma into her finely tuned olfactory system. She had performed this routine hundreds of times at MDD and, judging by her fervent tail-wagging, she seemed thrilled to be back in action.

In a clear voice I then said, "Seek . . . seek!"—the command to find the cat scent—before letting her off the leash.

Within fifteen minutes, Molly had searched an area the size of a soccer field and then, at the entrance of a small potting shed, she suddenly flung her body to the ground and performed the "down," her trademark "found it" signal, which she'd been taught at MDD.

I've done my job, Dad . . . she seemed to be saying, focusing her eyes on mine.

"Brilliant work, Molly," I said, my upbeat gestures causing her to leap three feet off the ground repeatedly

(I called these her "super-jumps"). Once she'd devoured her much-deserved reward, I gave her an extended play session with her favorite tennis ball, which was becoming balder by the day.

Each practice search at the farm became a new learning experience for both of us. Every session had a different objective—a trickier hiding place, maybe, or different weather conditions—and, slowly but surely, I increased their intensity and duration.

I also began to use real-life cats. Before I could deploy her on genuine missing-pet cases, I needed to be completely sure that Molly behaved appropriately in their presence and remained suitably calm, quiet and discreet.

"Would you mind awfully if I borrowed Pepper for a couple of hours?" I'd ask a friend, assuring them that their cat would be kept safe and secure and would at no point be released from its carrier. I would then hide the cat in a stable or hay barn for a bouncing Molly to locate in due course.

I captured many of these searches on a GoPro camera, which I'd strap to my chest, trying my best to keep up with Molly. I would analyze the footage afterward, focusing in on any achievements that could be repeated or any slipups that could be eliminated (on my part as well as my dog's). Then I would email the video clips to Mark at Medical Detection Dogs for his comments; occasionally, I'd follow this up with a visit to MDD, where he'd assess Team Molly's searching skills and attempt to iron out any glitches. This level of scrutiny could be immensely daunting; sometimes I felt like a reality show contestant whose every move was judged and critiqued by the resident expert.

Molly's success rate was phenomenal—she, memorably, found one cat sample deep in the base of a hollow fruit tree, where it had fallen after I'd hidden it much higher—and on the rare occasions that she failed to complete the scent match it was generally my fault. Once, I accidentally mixed up the samples, and another time I failed to sterilize the jar properly, effectively exposing Molly to two different cat scents. I always knew when I got something wrong because Molly would make a strange whining sound and sit down before me, as if to say, *Come on, Dad, get your act together* . . .

A real sense of solidarity started to grow between Molly and me, and that vital circle of trust began to strengthen. I had always wanted to emulate the man-and-dog teamwork I'd witnessed in my past. I'd seen the joy and satisfaction you can derive from bringing the best out of an animal and by maximizing its natural-born talents. Success relied on working as a team and trusting each other implicitly.

Forty years had passed since I'd helped my grandfather's friend on his sheep farm as a boy, but Alec's words of advice remained lodged in my psyche.

"An animal's love, trust and loyalty aren't given freely or easily, young man," he'd told me. "They have to be earned."

As Molly grew in confidence, both indoors and outdoors, I decided to take her on some selected work assignments—they were sort of "bring your dog to work" days. I chose appropriate dog-friendly venues to meet my private-eye clients, advising them beforehand that, if they wished to continue using my investigation services, there'd more often than not be a lovely cocker spaniel at my heel. Most of them were very accommodating and were super-kind to Molly, although I'm sure a few thought I'd completely lost it.

Molly, as it happened, became a useful asset, a nifty sidekick and my canine equivalent of Sherlock Holmes's Dr. Watson. If I needed to observe a specific house or office, for example, or survey a particular neighborhood, it was much easier to blend in if I was casually dressed and walking a dog on a lead. As a private eye, you had to become part of the environment and to look as if you belonged there and, with a cute dog at your side, suspicions were much less likely to be aroused.

Some canine-loving crooks would even strike up a conversation.

Molly's presence undoubtedly helped me to break down barriers and lower people's guards, and she also assisted me with my general pet-detective work, often acting as a smokescreen if I was investigating a fraudulent animal charity or a negligent boarding kennel. She accompanied me on a couple of missing-cat searches, too, the incidences of which were increasing as the temperatures rose and more pets ventured outdoors. I didn't ask her to perform any scent matching, though, and chose not to advertise her special abilities to my clients, my rationale being that we were in the midst of our skills training at Bramble Hill and still had much to absorb and refine.

Essentially, I still needed to establish Molly's safe parameters or—as I sometimes referred to it—her "operational envelope," a term I'd become familiar with while flying with the Royal Navy. For instance, how effective would my dog be when she was searching in built-up areas, as opposed to open ground? Could she search in wet conditions or snow? How many breaks would she need, and for how long? These, as well as other factors, could have an impact on her ability to find and match the scent of a missing cat.

One thing I knew for sure: Molly's unique talent

could be used only when both she and I were good and ready. Within a few weeks, that was indeed the case, and Molly and I would find ourselves experiencing our first real live search, successfully locating Rusty on that momentous February afternoon.

8

PHILLIP, HOLLY AND MISCHIEVOUS MOLLY

Once Molly had lived in Cranleigh for six weeks, it began to dawn on Sarah that this frisky young cocker spaniel was a permanent fixture, not a passing phase. In the blink of an eye we'd morphed into a household of three. This huge upheaval hadn't been easy for Sarah—Molly could be demanding and disruptive, similar to many change-resistant rescue dogs—and I could hardly blame her for feeling somewhat sidelined. My new dog had commanded my attention and sapped my spare time.

By the same token, though, Sarah genuinely appreciated my love for Molly—as well as my longtime passion for the cat-detection project—and so had shown remarkable patience. Especially since she was the first to admit that she wasn't a natural dog-lover. Sarah didn't even make that much of a fuss when Molly gnawed the heels of her brand-new boots; she just quietly presented me with a bill for a replacement pair.

"I know this has been hard for you, Sarah, and I know your nose has been pushed out of joint a bit," I said as we curled up together on the sofa one evening while Molly lay on the Persian rug chewing her favorite toy.

"Well, there's the understatement of the year," she replied with a wry smile.

"I do think Molly's behavior's improving, though, darling. She's starting to feel so much more settled now, and those teething problems seem few and far between."

"Mmmm . . . maybe . . ."

I affectionately ruffled my girlfriend's long blond hair.

And just then Molly suddenly regurgitated a wad of part-chewed grass and spat it out onto the rug. "Molly, that's gross." I frowned, rolling up a newspaper to shovel the gunky green mess. Sarah just sighed and shook her head. Molly looked up at us both, probably wondering what all the fuss was about.

There was no doubting that my dog still detected a certain coolness from the other female in the house. As the weeks had passed, I'd watched with interest as she'd tried—and generally failed—to worm her way into Sarah's affections, following her around the house or staring wistfully at her in an attempt to break the deadlock.

Okay, lady, so I know I'm not going to get the same attention from you that I get from Dad, she seemed to say, her eyes saucer-wide, *but how could you possibly not love a dog like me?*

╱ ╴ ╴ ╲ ╴ ╱

As the head of one of the UK's foremost pet-detective agencies, I was accustomed to receiving a variety of media requests. News outlets would often interview me about my line of work or ask for my comments regarding contemporary pet-related issues.

Sam and I occasionally arranged for some of UKPD's successful cases to appear in the local press and in pet magazines, too, which would print articles alongside photos of beaming owners cuddling their recently recovered fur-babies. It was a win-win situation, really; fifteen minutes of fame for my clients and their pets, feel-good content for the respective publications and fabulous PR for my service.

Radio and television also came knocking, and in early 2017 I received a request to appear on a long-time, successful daytime TV show. It was an opportunity I surely couldn't refuse.

"We're running a piece on the rise of dog thefts in the UK, Colin," explained the program researcher, "and we'd really appreciate some insight and opinion from a proper pet detective."

The hosts would interview me on set, and there'd also be a live feed to a former client of mine, Hayley, whose pet Chihuahua had been snatched the previous October. Mouse (so named because of her size) had eventually been recovered thanks to a painstaking UKPD investigation.

"Sounds great," I replied. "I'd be delighted to come on."

Sam agreed to take care of Molly while I was in London—my colleague would be glued to the TV at Bramble Hill Farm, no doubt—and I began to look forward to my appearance.

The day before the interview, however—not long after I'd returned from a very muddy practice search with Molly—I received another telephone call from the researcher. It turned out that one of the *This Morning* guests had canceled, and in order to fill the gap they'd decided to allocate more time to the canine-theft feature.

"We've given you a double slot now, so we were wondering whether you'd like to bring your dog, Molly, along with you as well?" she asked. "I hear she's a bit special—finds cats, doesn't she?—and I'm sure our viewers would *love* her."

I was somewhat thrown off by this conversation, and *umm*ed and *aaah*ed for a few moments before I made up my mind. While Molly's trailblazing recovery of Rusty had caused a few ripples via word of mouth,

I genuinely hadn't realized that news of her unique talent had spread further afield. It was my intention to shield Molly from the media spotlight for the time being, since I wanted us to have a few more successful searches under our belt and my dog still had much to learn. Despite maintaining this low profile, though, I'd still had to deflect inquiries from local reporters who'd heard rumors about a pet detective and his amazing rescue cocker spaniel. Some had become aware of our partnership when, during Molly's stint at MDD, the center had put out requests to local people for cat-hair samples, causing the journalists to dig a little deeper.

"So what d'you reckon, Colin?" badgered the researcher. "Is it a possibility? I need to let the director know in the next few minutes, you see . . ."

"Oh, go on, then," I said, perhaps against my better judgment.

"You don't need to worry," she said. "We've had many pets and animals on the show, so we're past masters at this."

As soon as I put the phone down I flung Molly straight into the bath. She couldn't meet the hosts of *This Morning* stinking of duck pond.

⟋ ⟋ ⟍ ⟍ ⟋

We arrived bright and early at the television studios the following day and were ushered straight into the

This Morning greenroom. I grabbed myself a coffee and soon started chatting with a fellow guest, a leading heart surgeon, who was extremely taken with Molly and appeared captivated by her story. Ten minutes into our conversation, however, a dog for the blind, Luna, and its handler had entered the greenroom—the program had been following the labradoodle puppy's progress for months, apparently—and the little cutie wanted to play with Molly. This was the last thing I needed. I had aimed to keep Molly totally calm before we went live on air and this puppy was beginning to wind her up.

"I think we need to keep them apart," I suggested to Luna's handler as both dogs barked at each other. "They're getting a bit too excited, aren't they?"

Fortunately, it was soon time for Luna to head to the studio, leaving behind a very hyper cocker spaniel and one very stressed owner.

Five minutes later a member of the production team directed us to another studio, which, being virtually identical to the main *This Morning* set, was used as a backup if there were any technical hitches and also as a holding area for guests prior to their broadcast slot. While it was a far quieter environment than the claustrophobic greenroom, any hopes of calming Molly down evaporated when a young runner on the show bounded in with a boxful of dog toys. No doubt he thought he was being helpful. My heart sank, however.

"I . . . I . . . I'd prefer it if you perhaps didn't show her those. She'll become overstimulated; she'll go bananas . . . ," I stuttered, my voice trailing off as I realized that the damage had already been done. Molly's hypersensitive nose had immediately detected the familiar smell of bendy rubber bones and fuzzy tennis balls and she was now geared up for some fun and games.

"No need to worry; there's plenty of space for her to play," grinned the runner, ignoring my grimace and cheerfully launching a ball across the room. "We've had loads of dogs in here."

Molly let out an excited yelp and hurtled toward her prey but came to an abrupt halt as she reached the full extent of her leash. She then performed a cartoonlike sprint-on-the-spot, straining to reach a pristine new tennis ball that was a couple of yards away. I had to slowly reel Molly back to the sofa, as if I were trying to land a giant fish.

"Lively, isn't she?" nodded the runner as I gave him a murderous stare.

Just at that moment the floor manager walked in, trailed by a cameraman holding his finger to his lips in a *ssshhhhh* gesture. A camera lens was shoved in my face and an audio feed boomed out from the adjacent studio.

"When we come back after the break we're going to

meet a real-life pet detective and his dog, Molly, who's been trained to find cats," said the familiar voice of Phillip Schofield. *This Morning* viewers then witnessed the camera panning to a fifty-something man with a sweaty brow and a stiff smile trying desperately to rein in a crazed cocker spaniel. It was an inauspicious start to our star turn on prime-time TV, and—believe me—it would only get worse.

"Time for you to have a quick chat with the presenters and to get you settled onto the sofa." The floor manager smiled and gestured for us to follow him.

My dog is anything but "settled," I felt like saying. *Thanks to Mr. Runner over there, my dog is as high as a bloody kite* . . .

Holly Willoughby was charming. She seemed genuinely pleased to see us—she was a dog-lover herself, telling me all about Benny, her French bulldog—and she made a point of thanking me for bringing along Molly at such short notice. Phillip, however, didn't appear quite so cordial. Granted, Molly continued to be jumpy and skittish (she was still hankering for the toys in the other studio) and I might have seemed slightly stressed, but he just looked on, silent and stony-faced, as I chatted with his co-presenter. No doubt his years of experience had alerted him to what looked like a very troublesome dog. All the while, I was trying to pacify Molly—I kept ruffling the nape of her neck and stroking her silken ears—but the little minx wasn't having any of it.

The ad break finished, the familiar *This Morning* jingle rang out and then we were live, beaming into the front rooms of millions of UK households. Phillip and Holly introduced me as a "real-life pet detective" and proceeded to quiz me about the rise in dog thefts, asking me how their viewers could best keep their pooches safe and secure. I advised against walking dogs at dusk—in my experience, many were stolen at this time of day—and suggested that animals should never be left alone in cars or town centers. I also emphasized the importance of training dogs to have excellent recall skills and recommended that owners should remain extra vigilant should there be a spate of thefts involving their specific breed.

"... and always contact the police in the first instance if you're convinced that your dog has been stolen," I added, "as they are obliged to investigate these cases."

They then quizzed me about Molly's ability to hunt out cats; I answered as succinctly as I could, but it was hard to remain focused with a wired and wide-eyed Molly straining at the leash. "What's she after?" asked Phillip, clearly concerned, when Molly began to whine loudly.

"She's after the dog toys from next door," I replied through gritted teeth.

"You can let her off her lead, if you like," suggested Holly. "She can go and play."

"Ooh, no, she wouldn't come back," I said with a nervous smile. "She'd get lost in the studios and I'd never see her again." They probably thought I was being precious, but what they didn't realize was that I rarely let Molly out of my sight—the only other people who walked Molly were Sarah, my son, Sam, and my colleague Sam—and the idea of her running amok in the cavernous South Bank studios filled me with dread.

As we soldiered on with the interview—with a frisky Molly attempting to climb onto the blue L-shaped sofa—I detected some unease behind the scenes. The director was concerned, apparently, that I was holding Molly too tightly on her leash—I really wasn't—and was fearful that it would prompt an avalanche of viewer complaints. I can only assume that a voice in Phillip's earpiece instructed him to take Molly off my hands, because he suddenly jumped up from the sofa and grabbed her lead.

"You two carry on, I'll look after Molly," he grinned, before taking her off the set and out of my eye-line. My protective instincts kicked in, and for a split second I contemplated running after Phillip and demanding my dog back. But then I realized I was in the middle of a live interview and that there was no other option but to keep calm and carry on. Beneath the cool veneer, however, I was panic-stricken.

Where's my dog? yelled a voice in my head. I visualized Phillip accidentally letting go of the leash and my precious cocker spaniel getting lost within the maze of corridors or becoming trapped inside an empty studio.

After a couple of torturous minutes—by then I was sweating from every pore—I spied a black flash of fluff darting back into the studio and diving underneath the sofa. A somewhat frazzled-looking Phillip followed in Molly's wake and reclaimed his seat next to Holly.

Phew, I thought. *Molly's safe.*

"... and let's now link up to a former client of Colin's, whose dog was targeted by thieves," said Phillip, as images of Hayley sitting at home in Hampshire with her tiny Chihuahua on her knee were beamed into the studio. Emotively and eloquently, she described

Mouse a few days after she was recovered

the traumatic chain of events that had led up to us finding Mouse.

As Hayley solemnly recounted her tale to the nation, however, she had to do so amid a soundtrack of grunts and snorts as Molly noisily explored the underside of the *This Morning* sofa. If that wasn't embarrassing enough, my dog then made a beeline for Holly and began to snuffle around the hem of her long, salmon-pink skirt.

The blond presenter burst out laughing.

"She's licking my feet!" she exclaimed, screwing up her face, while Hayley—who didn't have a clue what was going on—looked totally bewildered.

"She likes you," I said, immediately regretting how drippy that must have sounded.

Molly jumped on the sofa and crept across the back of it, her leash dragging after her. She then skulked behind Phillip and Holly, thwacking their necks with her long black tail as they attempted to read the teleprompter. And yes, the studio hands and camera operators may well have been guffawing, but I was dying inside. Molly had been billed as a supremely professional, highly trained detection dog, yet here she was, acting like an ill-disciplined toddler.

"Honestly, she doesn't do this at home," I said feebly, but I doubt anyone in the studio believed me.

"Talk about a scene-stealer," tutted Phillip, before,

inevitably, winding up the interview. "Thank you very much, Colin; it's been lovely meeting you," he said, but I wasn't that sure he meant it.

As we drove home, Molly sleeping soundly in the back of the car—and my blood pressure slowly returned to normal—I called Sarah. A peal of giggles rang out through my speakerphone.

"Tell me the truth, Sarah. It was a disaster, wasn't it?" I said.

"Not at all," she replied, once she'd finally stopped laughing.

"It was brilliant television, Colin. Molly was hilarious, and I bet the viewers *loved* it."

"You sure about that?"

"'Course. Molly was the funny, slapstick one and you were the serious straight man. Honestly, it was TV gold."

I spent the rest of the journey home reflecting on a bizarre morning and—much as it pained me—questioning my own judgment. I concluded that, in hindsight, I probably should have left Molly at home and out of the limelight. I had wanted to show her off, I suppose, like a proud parent, but by doing this I'd overlooked the fact that, deep down, she was still an excitable young rescue dog and was naturally prone to

mischief. She, like many pets, was never going to com-
ply with the rules and regulations of a live TV studio
and it had been unfair of me to expect anything more.

"I'm so sorry, Molls," I lamented as her snores rattled
around her crate.

Fast-forward a few hours, however, and it became
apparent that Sarah's judgment had been spot-on.
Molly's antics had hit it out of the park with the *This
Morning* viewers and, much to my surprise, had also
gone viral on the internet. Footage of my dog creating
havoc had been posted on the show's YouTube channel.

That same evening, Sarah and I watched the interview again (I spent most of the time peeping through
my fingers, I admit). Molly lay spread-eagle on the rug
by my feet, having enjoyed a long, bracing walk in the
woods followed by a bowl of her favorite dinner.

"Once a drama queen, always a drama queen,
Molly," I remarked as she looked up at me with her
brown eyes and raised a quizzical eyebrow, as if to say,
I can't help it if people love me . . .

As we continued to watch TV, I noticed with interest that my dog was attempting, slowly but surely, to
cozy up to Sarah. My girlfriend's attitude toward her
still wavered between tolerance and ambivalence, but
Molly was in no mood to abandon her charm offensive.
I couldn't help but smile as I watched her rest her chin
on Sarah's left sock and lean her head against her ankle,

edging as close as she could before Sarah noticed and peevishly moved her legs away.

"Mark my words, you two will be cuddled up on this sofa one day." I grinned.

"Not a chance," scowled Sarah. "I'll leave all that stuff up to you. I'd prefer not to have dog hairs on my trousers, thank you very much."

Molly padded back to me, somewhat resignedly, and curled up on the rug.

Don't give up, sweetheart, I felt like saying to her. *She'll come around in the end, I just know it . . .*

I felt it was important that we kept up our search momentum—it would boost Molly's confidence, as well as my own—so when, a few weeks later, Sam took a call about a missing cat, I was anxious to follow it up.

The client in question, Cat Jarvis (yes, her real name), worked as a press officer for Cats Protection, a well-known cat charity, and had called the office in a state of blind panic, so much so that she could barely speak. Eventually, Sam managed to decipher that Phoenix, a beautiful Bengal pedigree, had disappeared without a trace four days previously. There always seemed to be an upsurge in such cases during March; the evenings were starting to become lighter, which meant that cats like Phoenix were staying outdoors for longer.

"He's trapped somewhere, I know it," wailed Cat, "and I'm so scared he's not going to survive."

Fortunately, I didn't have any casework planned that morning, so I was able to prioritize this as an emergency. An average week for us usually entailed about twenty new inquiries; some were time-sensitive—what I call "fast track" investigations—and others fell into the category of protracted or "slow burn" cases. I usually tried to have six investigations running at the same time, allocating my time to each one as and when it was needed, always keeping some time back to respond promptly to any crisis calls like Cat's. On top of this, I also had to ensure that Stefan kept me informed on the progress of our private-eye cases, many of which would run for several months at a time. This meant that I'd often work a six-day week, which wasn't exactly ideal.

Sam, Molly and I made the short trip to our client's home and when she answered her front door, she promptly collapsed into my colleague's arms, her body shaking with sobs. While we were accustomed to dealing with traumatized owners, this lady was in a state of acute distress. She was dazed, disheveled and deathly white—the loss of her cat had clearly hit her hard.

It being a fast-tracked case, I'd not had the opportunity to obtain any background information from the owner. In an ideal situation, I'd have a thirty-minute telephone conversation with the client, obtaining details about the missing pet's health, diet, temperament, daily activity and behavior toward other pets and people. This fact-finding usually served to help me decide whether or not to take on a case and would also help me to select the best possible strategy. In this instance, however, the lack of context meant that we would be going in cold—not my preferred approach, by any means, but if Phoenix was trapped in a building (as her owner suspected), we needed to locate him as soon as possible.

Judging by Cat's emotional state, I realized that we'd have to address her trauma before we were able to get any meaningful details about Phoenix and the circumstances of his disappearance. It was at times such as these that my policing experience came into play.

I had learned over the years that some human brains found it hard to differentiate between the trauma of a missing child and a missing pet, and for that reason I applied exactly the same counseling techniques. I would give my clients the opportunity to pour out their grief and express their fears and, having unburdened themselves, they'd soon become calmer and more rational. With tact and diplomacy, I'd then ask the questions that would allow me to build up a picture of the pet's personality and preferences and enable me to start coordinating the search. Usually, I could extract this kind of information only once their emotions were in check.

The one downside of this person-centered approach was that the client would often transfer their hopes and fears onto me, which would ramp up the pressure to get a result.

"I'm counting on you to end this nightmare. You're my last resort," was a common response.

This was exactly what happened with Cat, who, in the living room of her 1930s home, cried herself dry and beseeched me to find Phoenix. She was in a state of emotional shutdown—and, unlike most clients of mine, she hadn't mustered the strength to cover the basics. Her house-to-house inquiries, her distribution of posters and her use of social media had been somewhat disorganized.

"Seems like we're starting from scratch here," I whispered to Sam.

I decided to employ a pinwheel-type search strategy that morning, starting from the inside and spiraling outward. I googled a map on my iPad, tagged Cat's house, plotted Phoenix's likely territory and identified the gardens and sheds in that area. I also took a sample of Phoenix's scent for Molly—our pièce de résistance, I hoped—in order to maximize the chances of recovery. My fragile client had dissolved into tears when she'd presented me with her pet's hair-covered blanket.

Contrary to my advice—I'd strongly suggested that she stay indoors—Cat insisted on accompanying us on the search around the village. ("It'll make me feel closer to him," she'd said.) Our first task was to conduct door-to-door inquiries. We showed neighbors a photo of Phoenix—he was a stunning-looking cat, with distinctive marbled, grayish-brown markings—before quizzing them about his whereabouts and trying to establish a pattern of behavior. I tried to speak to as many neighbors and witnesses as possible.

"When did you last see him?" I'd ask. "Do you spot him regularly? And what time of day, roughly? Does he have a favorite little haven in your garden? Have you seen him with other cats?"

One particular front door was answered by a young woman in a dressing gown who took one look at me, then one at Molly, and gasped in shock.

"Oh my goodness!" she cried, before dashing to the foot of her stairs. "Kids, get out of bed, you'll never believe who's at our front door."

A pair of drowsy, pajama-clad children appeared at their mother's side, rubbing their eyes. They soon shook themselves awake when they saw the dog on the doorstep, though.

"*It's Molly!*" they squealed in unison. "*Molly the naughty dog!*" The kids and their mom were among the millions of viewers who'd seen Molly's exploits on TV just a few weeks earlier. I allowed them to pet and stroke her for a couple of minutes—she adored the attention—and it was quite touching to see the children's joyful reaction. Molly's celebrity status was growing, it seemed.

"You'll have to get used to playing second fiddle, Colin," said a laughing Sam. "Molly's the star of the show now."

Once all the fan-worshipping had calmed down and the kids had returned to their bedroom, we asked about Phoenix.

"Oh, I know that cat. He's a gorgeous little thing," said the woman. "He usually crawls under my privet hedge and sits there for an hour or so, but I'm afraid I've not seen him since the weekend."

Other neighbors had similar accounts—he'd often sit on number 12's fence to observe a bird table and would bask on number 23's patio when the sun shone—but there'd been no recent sightings. This information—coupled with the fact that Molly hadn't detected a strong enough scent in any of their gardens—led me to believe that one of three things had happened. Phoenix had either been trapped, accidentally transported out of the area or killed. For Cat's sake, I dearly hoped it wasn't the latter.

After a pause for lunch we resumed the search. I re-introduced Phoenix's scent to Molly and as we ambled down a wide, leafy avenue, I noticed her becoming a little animated. Her trot quickened and her tail-wagging increased as we passed a huge fenced and gated property with a large, square garden and a couple of swanky cars in the driveway.

Seeing this house gave me a sudden, jarring flashback to the case of Oscar, the scared and skinny cat I'd found cowering in the garden shed of a similar house. I'd always felt that I'd not located Oscar quickly enough—and my shortcomings had been the catalyst for finding a cat-detection dog like Molly. The fact that I was now working in tandem with this very dog, in order to try and rescue a cat in peril, felt both surreal and satisfying.

This is exactly why I've got Molly, I said to myself. *I can't go through another case like Oscar's. I need to get into this garden, pronto . . .*

With my dog getting more agitated by the second—she clearly had the scent in her nostrils—I walked over to the property's tall black gate and pressed the buzzer. No reply. I pressed it again, and again; still no reply. It was only when I leaned on the buzzer for a good twenty seconds that a voice finally crackled through the intercom.

"Will you please stop ringing the bell?" barked a woman. "The residents aren't in at the moment."

"Sorry about that—I think there's a problem with

Molly indicating that she had found a missing animal.

your buzzer—but we're looking for a lost cat, you see, and a neighbor has seen it run into your garden."

It wasn't big, and it wasn't clever, but I often had to tell little white lies to gain access.

"I wish I could help, love, but I'm not allowed to let anyone in. I'm afraid I'm going to have to ask you to come back when the owners are home."

I wasn't taking no for an answer. There was no way that I was leaving until I searched this garden; Molly was indicating that Phoenix was close by and if he was trapped somewhere, we needed to find him as soon as possible.

Somehow I had to get this person to the gate; it was never easy to tug on somebody's heartstrings via intercom. I pressed hard on the buzzer for another twenty seconds.

"Will you *please* stop ringing the bloody bell?" she shouted. "You can't come in, I've told you."

"I'm not touching it," I lied, yelling over the incessant buzzing. "As I said, it appears to be stuck. I think you'll find it needs repairing."

"Oh, bloody Nora, just wait there," I heard, and the intercom clicked off.

My dastardly ploy had worked. The front door opened and a small, squat, dark-haired woman emerged, dressed in chef's whites. The occupants' personal cook, I assumed.

"You know what, I think I may have fixed it for you," I said as she advanced toward us, wearing a puzzled expression. "This was jammed into the button," I fibbed, showing her a small metal washer that I'd fortuitously found on the pavement. "Bloody kids, eh? Anyway, as I was saying . . ."

Then, before the little chef had the chance to scuttle off, I regaled her with the story of poor Phoenix and his perturbed owner and explained how Molly (who by now was whining in frustration) had detected a possible scent trail. Somehow, I managed to twist her arm—her sympathetic nods suggested she was a cat-lover herself—and she eventually unbolted the gate.

"But you'd better be quick," she said. "My bosses have been on a cruise and they're due back tonight."

I let Molly off the lead and she shot across the lawn

like a cannonball. She then leaped up acrobatically, arching her back, inhaling the air, gauging the scent source. My heart thumped when she veered off toward the westerly side of the garden and pelted toward the brick-built garage. Rarely had I seen her so focused. This was Molly on a mission.

Please let Phoenix be in there, I said to myself, following in her drag. *And please let him be alive.*

As I lifted open the giant garage double doors—they were unlocked, luckily—a waft of air hit my face, bringing with it the overpowering stench of cat pee. Within a millisecond, a quivering Molly had done the "down"—no surprise there—but, to the naked eye, there was neither sight nor sound of Phoenix. Not helping matters was the fact that the garage was full of clutter, from floor to ceiling. With Molly remaining still and silent, just as she'd been trained to do, I gently started to move the teetering items of furniture. I did so very gingerly, however, since I was petrified that it was all going to come noisily tumbling down, like a giant game of Jenga. As I gradually cleared some space, I must have released a vacuum of cat scent, because Molly suddenly slid over to the back of the garage and gave me another definitive "down." This time she also wiggled her bottom and shuffled her paws, which was usually a surefire sign of certitude.

I'm absolutely positive the cat is here, my dog was saying. *One hundred percent . . .*

With Cat at my side, and Sam and the chef looking on, I slowly crept toward Molly, moved an old, dusty golf bag to one side and—lo and behold—behind it sat Phoenix. The way he defensively sprang up, arched his back and hissed in anger told me he was very much alive and well.

I think the whole town must have heard his owner's shrieks of joy.

Afterward, the four of us stood among all that garage junk, chatting and laughing, as Phoenix cocooned himself in Cat's arms, thoroughly relieved to be back with his mom. Molly, meanwhile, spun around in tight circles, panting and squeaking, almost in celebratory fashion.

Uplifting outcomes like these made me realize exactly why I'd trained Molly in the first place: to save cats' lives, to help distraught owners who could barely think straight and, ultimately, to reunite them with their lost pets. They had been my main objectives from day one, and to see everything come to fruition like this was simply marvelous.

News of my dog's brilliant cat-detecting exploits began to spread like wildfire—some local press coverage of Molly had been picked up by national newspapers—and, soon enough, we both received an invitation to attend Crufts, the world-famous canine show and exhibition. We had been asked to represent Medical Detection Dogs—an honor, of course, considering everything that Claire, Rob and Mark had done for us—and we'd also be the VIP guests of Natural Instinct, a well-known dog food manufacturer.

"We're so pleased you're both coming," gushed a press officer who called to confirm our three-day attendance at Birmingham's National Exhibition Center. She seemed enchanted by our story (". . . a rescue dog that became a cat's best friend . . . how *wonderful*!") and she informed me that they'd already received dozens of interview requests from print and broadcast media, both national and international, many prompted by the *This Morning* footage.

"In fact, Channel 4 has been in touch this morning . . . they want to film Molly at Bramble Hill Farm and are wondering whether you would like to take part in a live chat on the sofa with Clare Balding?"

As she asked the question, an image of Molly slobbering over Holly Willoughby's ankle briefly flashed before me. I assumed that Crufts would be an entirely different proposition, however. I'd learned a lot from my TV experience, and this time around I'd make sure that both Molly and I were much better prepared for the media attention.

"Count us in," I told the press officer. "It would be an absolute privilege."

On the day of the broadcast Molly and I traveled north to Birmingham, meeting up with my good friend Anna. Having worked extensively in canine-related PR and broadcasting, she'd suggested I draft a press release detailing Molly's journey from rescue dog to sniffer dog—including her brilliant recoveries of Rusty and Phoenix—which she'd roll out to the media in advance of the show. We wouldn't be able to fulfill every interview request—and I was reluctant to overwork and overwhelm Molly—so this was a good way of keeping everyone informed and updated.

As a result of this, the media buzz surrounding Molly was incredible and she was treated like a celebrity. Reporters were as keen to meet my charismatic little spaniel as they were to meet some of the show dogs and wherever we went in the exhibition hall, we were stopped by people asking for selfies, photographs or cuddles (with Molly, of course, not me; I'd generally hover in the background, like her minder). She absolutely loved all the attention and adulation.

"What a clever, clever wee lassie," cooed a tweed-suited Scottish lady, gently stroking her head. "I've got three Persians back in Dundee, and I'd be heartbroken if any of them went missing. So keep up the good work, Molly, hun."

It was during Channel 4's prime-time 8 p.m. slot, on the first day of Crufts, that we met Clare Balding on the sofa. She would be interviewing me, together with the CEO and co-founder of MDD, Claire Guest. This time I was determined that Molly would behave herself, bearing in mind that we were broadcasting live to an audience of millions of dog-lovers in the UK and across the globe.

I was already a huge fan of Clare's—she is a talented writer and a superb TV presenter—and I found her really warm and friendly. She made a big fuss of Molly prior to the show and was highly amused when Molly tried to pilfer some of the food that the crew had hidden behind the sofa for her.

"I've hardly stopped all day, and I'm starving," she grinned, tucking into her sandwich as Molly looked up at her with doleful eyes.

"Here, have a snack, greedy guts," I added, giving Molly a handful of her favorite beef-jerky bites, "and keep your paws off Clare's dinner."

With twenty minutes to go before we went on air, however, my dog began to get worryingly frisky and I started to break out into a cold sweat. Fortunately, I had expert assistance on hand. The rest of the team from Medical Detection Dogs had left their exhibition stand to watch the filming—Rob and Mark included—and the latter was able to apply some simple calming techniques. "Just walk her around, Colin, away from the crowds, and quietly chat to her. This should help to remove the anxiety. She can probably sense that you're also stressed, don't forget, so you need to stay chilled, too."

As it happened, I couldn't have hoped for a better interview. Clare was as professional as ever—she'd clearly done her research on scent-detecting canines—and Molly behaved impeccably throughout, snuggling next to me on the sofa and curiously eyeing the crowd of Crufts visitors that had amassed around the makeshift studio. As the show was beamed out to its worldwide audience, I talked about Molly's rescue-dog origins, explaining how I'd given this disadvantaged animal another chance at happiness and how she'd reciprocated by offering me love, loyalty and companionship. By investing my time, patience and dedication, not only had Molly been transformed into a scent-detection prodigy, she had also become a much-adored pet. Clare put me at ease throughout; indeed, it felt more like a conversation between friends than an interview.

"Time to see this fantastic dog in action," she said, cueing up the short film that had been captured at Bramble Hill Farm a few weeks earlier. On a nearby monitor, I watched the footage of Molly taking the feline scent sample and bombing over to a derelict barn to locate my neighbor's cat in its carrier, just as she'd been trained to do.

"Wow," whispered Clare. "I've never seen anything like it."

I glanced over at Rob and Mark, both of whom were beaming with pride.

I knew exactly how they felt. Our Molly was a super-star.

9

BRING BACK BUFFY

As a pet detective, I've handled hundreds of dog-theft cases. Over the last decade, sadly, it's become a colossal problem in the UK, largely due to the growing popularity of valuable "designer dogs," as well as the increasingly sophisticated methods of merciless thieves. It's a heinous, heartless crime.

When Molly and I had first joined forces, I continued to take on the occasional missing-dog investigation. I was very selective, however, and would agree to offer my services only if I felt confident that my safety, and that of my dog or my staff, would not be compromised. One such case will live forever in my memory.

In April 2017 I was contacted by a Sri Lankan woman, Renu, who informed me that her seventeen-week-old pet had been stolen from her house in a north London suburb. Buffy, a beautiful white, golden-eared puppy—a rare cross-breed known as a Coton de

A fluffy Buffy before she was stolen

Tulear—had been snatched one Friday evening while Renu had been dining at a local restaurant with her husband, Sachin, and her two sons, Harry and Freddie.

When they'd returned home, at about ten o'clock, Sachin's blue BMW 5 Series was missing from the driveway.

"Renu, the car's gone," he'd said. "They must've gone inside to get the keys."

"Oh my god . . . oh my god . . . *BUFFY!*" his wife had screamed.

She had raced around to the back of the property, only to be confronted with a gaping patio door, which the robbers had forced open. In the sitting room, she'd discovered an ominously empty dog bed, in which Buffy had been snoozing contentedly when they'd gone for their meal. A frantic search of the house had revealed no trace of her whatsoever. Not only had these coldhearted burglars ransacked the property and stolen money, handbags and jewelry—as well as the car, of course—in all likelihood, it seemed they had also abducted an innocent puppy. The family was utterly devastated. The sweet, lovable Buffy had become a huge part of their lives—almost like a third child to Renu and Sachin and a sibling to the boys—and the idea of her being alone, in danger, was just too awful for them to contemplate. To make matters worse, the response from the Metropolitan Police hadn't exactly been encouraging. The officers who arrived on scene the following day had been quite dismissive of the idea that the thieves had stolen the family dog.

"She's probably just run off," they'd shrugged, treating Buffy's disappearance with the same level of concern as they were Renu's missing handbag. "Give it a few days and she'll probably turn up in a neighbor's garden."

Friends and neighbors rallied around them, launching a "Bring Back Buffy" campaign on social media, registering her details on the DogLost website and helping to display posters and distribute flyers. Renu's plight even attracted the attention of the newspaper the *Evening Standard*: DEVASTATED MOTHER OFFERS REWARD AFTER PUPPY IS SNATCHED, ran the headline.

The publicity raised much-needed awareness and led to numerous reports of a "white, fluffy dog" in their area. Agonizingly for Renu, none of these pooches turned out to be Buffy; her hopes would soar with each promising sighting, only to be cruelly dashed when it became clear that these dogs were doppelgängers.

Time quickly passed, and by the time May had arrived the family had begun to lose all hope of ever seeing their cherished puppy again. It was during a chance conversation with Buffy's breeder, however, that Renu had discovered that there was another option to pursue.

"My friend's dog was recovered by a pet detective, a guy based near Guildford," she'd said. "Why not get in touch with him? I mean, you've got nothing to lose, have you?"

Within hours she'd accessed my website and given me a call.

Molly and I found ourselves knocking on Renu's door the following afternoon. An elegant brunette in her late thirties, Renu gave me a kiss on both cheeks—and Molly a hug—before ushering us into her bright, airy front room. Sitting on the sofa in their school uniforms were her sons, Harry and Freddie. Their eyes lit up like candles when my dog trotted in, sporting her usual wide, pink-tongued doggy grin.

"Aw, she's *soooooo* cute," said Harry, the elder of the two, holding out his hand for Molly to snuffle while his younger brother chuckled beside him.

"I tell you what, lads, why don't you take her into the back garden for a run-around?" I smiled, winking conspiratorially at Renu. "She always needs to stretch her legs if she's been in the car a while."

"Really? Can we?" asked Harry, slightly tentatively.

"Of course," I replied, lobbing over Molly's favorite tennis ball.

I didn't want the boys to know that I'd brought her with me for a reason. During our phone call, Renu had revealed how much they'd both bonded with Buffy and how anguished they'd been following her disappearance. Her younger son, Freddie, had reacted particularly badly, so much so that he'd made his mom promise that she wouldn't replace her with another dog. It would only get snatched by "nasty men," like before, he'd said, and this would make him feel "all sad and lonely" again. It had broken his mother's heart, and she had hoped that a little canine therapy, courtesy of a cute cocker spaniel, might help the healing process.

As I watched Harry and Freddie dash down the garden after Molly, I was instantly reminded of myself and my brother David at a similar age, hot on the heels of our own family dog. My brother and I would have been utterly devastated had our beloved pooch been so cruelly snatched from us, and I felt so sorry for these poor young boys. It seemed horribly unfair.

With her sons out of earshot, Renu and I were able to address more serious matters. She ran through the events surrounding Buffy's disappearance, gulping down sobs as she revisited the awful memories of that fateful day.

"It's the worst thing that's ever happened to me, Colin," she said, shaking her head. "I don't give a hoot that the thieves have stolen the car and my jewelry, to be honest—they're replaceable—but I can't come to terms with the fact that they've taken my Buffy. My gorgeous puppy. My precious baby. Who would do such a thing?"

"Here, have a tissue," I whispered as her face crumpled and the tears streamed down her cheeks. I had comforted plenty of distraught dog-lovers over the years, yet witnessing their grief and suffering never got any easier. This poor woman was utterly broken.

"The thing is, I know there are some people out there who think I'm overreacting, and who'll say, 'It's only a dog,'" she continued. "But they tend not to be pet owners. They think that unconditional love is just reserved for humans. They just don't understand."

I heard a bark from the back garden and craned my neck to check that Molly was okay. A giggling Harry was holding the ball aloft, teasing his doggy playmate, but Freddie was leaning against the wall with his head down and his hands deep in his pockets. My heart went out to the younger boy—I could read his mind—and it was at that very moment that I decided to take on the case. Since Molly's arrival, UKPD had focused primarily on finding missing cats, but Buffy's case had touched me. The pup's theft was hurting every member of this lovely family, and I believed I was the best chance they had of ever seeing her again. I was very careful to manage Renu's expectations, however.

Buffy had been missing for over three months and with each passing day, the chances of finding her were becoming slimmer. I also knew that it would be an extremely difficult investigation and that I was going to need a few lucky breaks along the way. On the plus side, I'd successfully investigated hundreds of burglaries as a police officer (I'd be deploying my full range of sleuthing skills to try and trace Buffy) and my success rate for recovering stolen dogs was excellent. Not only that, I'd also have my intrepid canine assistant by my side. While Molly hadn't been trained to scent-match dog odors, she was more than able to help me with site searches, and—as she'd done many times previously—would be acting as a decoy during surveillance operations.

"I think of Molly as the Watson to my Sherlock," I said, which elicited a little smile from Renu. "And one thing's for sure: we're going to do all we can to bring Buffy home."

The following day I printed up some photos of the missing dog, as well as a stack of business cards featuring my contact details. For each investigation, I would use a different pay-as-you-go cell phone, a practice that I'd originally introduced to the private-eye side of my business but which I'd also decided to employ as a pet detective.

My first task was to establish, with as much certainty as possible, that Buffy hadn't escaped during the burglary. With this in mind, I roamed the streets of the area and spoke to as many local residents as possible, focusing particularly on dog walkers. Having the ever-friendly Molly with me made this infinitely easier—she was a brilliant ice breaker—and I was able to strike up a number of useful conversations. None of the walkers, it transpired, had seen this distinctive little puppy on the evening of the burglary, or indeed, ever since. One close neighbor, a Barbour-jacketed gentleman with an elderly Airedale terrier, was particularly obliging.

"I walk my Jerry every night, between nine o'clock and eleven, and I go right past the lady's house," he said. "It's almost like I'm on sentry patrol—I stroll up and down the same road, at the same time—and

I'm pretty certain I'd have seen that little dog running about."

"Thanks," I said as Molly and Jerry bumped noses. "You've been really helpful."

His testimony—as well as the total lack of sightings of this distinctive dog—convinced me that the thieves had left the scene with Buffy in tow. And as I began to build up a picture of the crime and draw up a profile of the thieves, I started to suspect that it had been a planned and professional theft, as opposed to an impromptu, ad-hoc raid. Having perhaps staked out the property for weeks, and aware that the family often went out on Fridays, the offenders had specifically targeted Sachin's car that evening. When they'd come across Buffy, however—and had realized she was a pup with a price tag—they'd decided to snatch her, too. I wondered whether this pretty little dog had been given to a gangster's wife, or a girlfriend, along with the handbags and the jewelry; it seemed quite odd that the household iPads and laptops had been ignored.

Due to a lack of forensic evidence at the crime scene and the failure to find the stolen BMW, within two weeks the police had gradually scaled down their inquiries. I wasn't prepared to give up that easily, though, despite the passage of time, and I planned to approach this case with the rigor and diligence it deserved. Anxious to obtain as much detail as possible, one morning I drove to north London to meet Renu's husband and, over tea for two at a dog-friendly café, he gave me his version of events. Molly sat dutifully by my side, flinching with excitement every time a new customer entered and the bell on the front door tinkled.

"One thing I should have mentioned to you, Colin, is that when the car was stolen the fuel tank was virtually empty," said Sachin. "I'm pretty sure the burglars would've needed to fill it up straightaway."

"Drink up your tea," I replied, galvanized by this golden nugget of information. "We're going on a garage crawl."

With Sachin in my passenger seat, and Molly in her dog crate, I visited a handful of local gas stations within a five-mile catchment area of the family home. Rogues and robbers rarely paid for fuel, so I asked each manager to check if they'd had any so-called "pump and runs" involving a blue BMW on the day of the burglary.

"You know what, I think we did . . . ," said one, flicking through a diary before stopping at the date in question. "Yeah, remember it well. They filled up a whole tank, then sped off. Three dark-haired lads. One getting the gas, two others sitting in the car. I've still got the CCTV if you want to take a look?"

"Absolutely we do," I said.

The footage provided two significant pieces of information. First, the registration plates had swiftly been removed, the plan being to replace them with fake plates. This—together with the fact they'd filled up the tank completely—suggested to me that the thieves intended to keep using the car themselves for the foreseeable future. Secondly, the images showed three young men—in their late teens, perhaps, or early twenties.

The net seemed to be closing in on our offenders, and I could only hope and pray that the BMW would soon resurface. Only then, I felt, would I get any nearer to cracking the case, and to discovering Buffy's fate.

While I continued to circulate images of the missing dog, a good two weeks passed without any major leads or developments. There was another maddening case of mistaken identity, sadly, whereby a dog answering Buffy's description (and with the same name, apparently) had been spotted by a passerby in a North London park. I had followed up the next day, with Molly and Sam in tow, but it had become quickly apparent that— pardon the pun—we were barking up the wrong tree. Not only was this dog much older and plumper (it actually looked more like a Maltese terrier), we also heard its owner yelling "Poppy . . . come here, Poppy!" when it had scampered past us.

"I suppose Poppy does sound a *little bit* like Buffy," shrugged Sam.

"Yeah, only if you're wearing earmuffs." I sighed. "Time to give Renu the bad news."

Our client was understandably crestfallen when I called her—she'd felt really optimistic about this particular sighting—but it seemed she had some news of her own to relay.

"You're not going to believe this, Colin, but Sachin's BMW has been found," she said, explaining that it had been abandoned following an accident and towed to the Met Police car pound. Officers had checked it for forensic evidence but had concluded there was nothing of significance.

"By rights, our car-insurance company owns it now," added Renu, "but they've agreed we can examine it, too, if we want, before it goes off to auction."

"That's *fantastic* news," I replied. "I'm on my way."

Sam took Molly home to Sussex, and I met Sachin at the car pound.

We were eventually ushered through a turnstile and into the pound itself. It was like a vast, out-of-town car supermarket, with line upon line of confiscated vehicles, ranging from flashy sports cars to total write-offs.

Sachin's BMW was clearly in the latter category. It was a mangled mess of metal—the crash had been high impact—and, I assumed, would be sold off for parts only.

As Sachin chatted with the clerk, I began to search the car's interior. Throughout my fourteen years as a police officer, I'd searched lots of stolen cars and every single search had resulted in the discovery of a crucial piece of evidence that had taken the investigation forward. You needed to be very thorough, and you needed to break the search down into four phases: trunk, hood, exterior and interior.

When I opened up the trunk I was surprised to find that it contained two new wheels (probably stolen) and a gas can. I could only assume that the thieves had not risked taking the car to any more gas stations and had opted to siphon their fuel from other cars. The presence of the two spare wheels suggested that the robbers were thinking about keeping the car for the foreseeable future.

The search of the hood, exterior and front interior drew a blank, however. It seemed I was dealing with a gang of professional crooks who had gone to a lot of trouble not to leave any forensic evidence behind that could lead to their identity.

Finally, I climbed into the rear passenger seats and had a good look around. Still nothing.

Come on, Colin, look harder, I berated myself. *There's always something . . .*

I cast my mind back to some of the previous searches I'd completed and remembered one occasion when I'd found a piece of evidence beneath the front passenger seat. Eager to comb every inch of Sachin's car, I decided to check the underside of Sachin's passenger seat, my heartbeat quickening when I felt something plastic and sticky. I gave it a gentle tug and when I realized what it was, could hardly believe my eyes. There in my hand was a parking ticket bearing a registration number, a date, a time and—crucially—a location: the northeast London suburb of Stoke Newington.

"*YESSSS!*" I whispered to myself, performing a covert little fist pump. This was the significant breakthrough I'd been waiting for, the stroke of luck that would allow my investigation finally to gather some momentum.

The clerk remained deep in conversation with my client so, while he wasn't looking, I furtively slipped the yellow notice into my pocket. A tad naughty of me, I suppose—I ought really to have informed the police—but the Met had shown little interest in this case and I figured I needed this cold, hard evidence more than they did.

Sachin was overjoyed with this momentous development—he realized how pivotal it could be—and after

I bade him farewell I set about following the first of many lines of inquiry. A check on the false license plate revealed that the thieves had cloned it from an identical BMW on sale in a Birmingham car dealership, confirming my suspicions that the burglary had been planned. I called the showroom manager, who said that he'd been somewhat perplexed by the deluge of parking tickets and court summonses he'd received recently. Due to data-protection law, however, he regretted he was unable to send me copies.

Undeterred, I asked Sachin to inform officials about the parking tickets related to his car and to ask if he could settle the payments online. Bingo. He was given a unique reference number which enabled him to access a grand total of five parking tickets online, all of which had been generated in the Stoke Newington area.

"I think I can hazard a guess as to where the thieves live," I said when he forwarded me the details.

Then, using my network of contacts, I identified, and then interviewed, the traffic wardens who had issued each parking ticket. They were legally obliged to take photographs of offending vehicles in order to provide evidence of time and location—some wardens captured video footage, too—and as a result our investigation took another major leap forward. The biggest break came in the form of two separate photos, which revealed background images of two men—mechanics, I presumed—who appeared to be working on roadside vehicles just yards away from where the BMW had been illegally parked.

These guys could be the best witnesses we've got, I thought to myself.

It was time to go undercover on the streets of northeast London. It was also time to draft in the assistance of Detective Constable Molly Butcher.

To secure the locals' trust (and to acquaint myself with the territory), I thought it would be wise for me to go incognito, so I ditched my UKPD fleece, donned my jeans and T-shirt, and posed as a regular guy, casually walking his cocker spaniel along Stoke Newington High Street. As ever, with the gregarious Molly by my side, it was much easier to blend into the crowd.

Armed with a wad of "Bring Back Buffy" leaflets, I visited various shops, cafés and businesses, introducing myself as Terry, a friend of Renu's who was raising awareness about the dog's disappearance.

"The family doesn't want to get anyone into trouble, and they're not aiming to involve the police. They just want Buffy back," I explained to the owner of a barber shop. (I was particularly focused on getting the message across that, should Buffy be recovered alive, there would be no repercussions.) Then I proceeded to tug gently on his heartstrings—a well-worn technique.

"The whole household is heartbroken, as you can imagine," I said as the barber nodded sympathetically. "My friend's worried sick, and her kids can hardly sleep at night. I don't know about you, mate, but I couldn't cope if my dog went missing."

The man looked down at Molly, who—as if on cue—tilted her head to one side and gazed imploringly at him. Meryl Streep would have been so proud.

"No, me neither. I'd be so, so upset," he said. "My French bulldog means everything to me. *Everything . . .*"

"Exactly," I replied, handing over a business card and a leaflet. "Please, if you have any information about Buffy's whereabouts, you must give me a call."

With my trusty sidekick trotting obediently at my heel, I continued with my door-to-door inquiries. Most people we met were very helpful and promised to keep their eyes peeled, but the total absence of sightings in the district suggested that the puppy was either being kept indoors, had been whisked out of the area or was no longer alive. While the prospect of the latter was far too grim to dwell upon, at the same time I had to be realistic: there was always a risk that thieves would see a dog as a liability—she directly linked them to their crime, after all. But that was the worst-case scenario, of course, and I was determined to stay positive.

"Come on, Molly." I smiled, heading off to a nearby park for some tennis ball–related fun and frolics. "You've worked incredibly hard today. Time for a well-earned break."

The following day I ramped things up a notch. Molly and I visited a handful of Stoke Newington community centers, hanging the Buffy posters in areas of busy foot traffic and maximum visibility. I'd also asked Sam to mock up a photo of Sachin's BMW, sporting the fake plates, which I brandished at every opportunity in the hope that it would jog someone's memory. Then, I revealed my true pet-detective identity to a number of well-connected individuals—council officers and café owners, for instance—before asking them to spread the word far and wide.

My strategy was to reach the thieves through the community and to apply pressure on them. *Give Buffy back* was my message, *and then I'll go away*. News would hopefully filter through to the perpetrators that I was on their case and that I was zeroing in on their community. I needed them to feel the pressure.

Outside one community hub I chatted with a middle-aged Jamaican woman walking a frisky, yappy Jack Russell terrier. Dressed in a rainbow-hued robe and matching head wrap, she listened intently as I gave her the lowdown on Buffy's story, from the missing dog to the mangled car. I also happened to show her the traffic warden's images of the mechanics by the roadside, whom I was keen to identify as potential witnesses.

"That looks very much like Mr. Wilson and his son," she said, giving her dog's leash a sharp tug as he dashed toward Molly. "They fix a lot of the cars in the neighborhood, including my husband's. Nice gentlemen, I'm sure they'll be happy to help. Let me give you directions . . ."

Mr. Wilson's place was sandwiched between two sprawling housing estates. As Molly and I walked past a sea of boarded-up shops and properties, many of them plastered with graffiti and posters, it seemed like a world apart from the bustling vibrancy of the main street, just a stone's throw away. Most passersby walked with their heads down—no nods or pleasantries here—and, rightly or wrongly, I felt myself holding Molly's lead extra tightly.

As I sidled over to Mr. Wilson's, a raucous game of dominoes was in mid-flow. Four middle-aged men were sitting around a table—an upturned oil drum, to be precise—whooping, laughing, groaning and backslapping as tiles were dramatically slapped down. One of them, wearing paint- and oil-spattered overalls, noticed me and Molly. I raised my palm in a *no, carry on, I'll wait* gesture.

Five minutes later the game had come to an end and three of the four men had gone their separate ways, leaving behind the man in the overalls.

"Mr. Wilson?" I asked, handing over my business card. "My name's Colin Butch—"

"The guy looking for the dog, yeah?" he interrupted. "My friend Rosie rang to say you might be paying me a visit."

I spent the next few minutes showing him all my photographic evidence. He confirmed that the traffic warden's image depicted him and his son—they often did roadside repairs in the area—and I asked him if he'd ever noticed the blue BMW or, better still, had completed any repair work on it. The vehicle had probably been in a few scrapes before the recent accident, I explained, and there appeared to be two new wheels in the trunk that were ready to be fitted.

His thumb and forefinger stroked the white bristles on his chin.

"I'm not aware of the car myself," he said, "but you might want to speak to my son about it."

I paused for a few moments, waiting for him to elaborate. "He takes on some jobs that I wouldn't touch with a barge pole," he sighed, "but some groups of lads can be, shall we say, a little persistent . . ."

His voice trailed off and he seemed unwilling to divulge any more details. Being a father myself, I recognized those protective, paternal instincts.

"I can promise you, Mr. Wilson, that no one's going to get into trouble. Buffy's owners would prefer not to involve the police. And it's my job to seek pets, not prosecutions."

My assurances seemed to relieve him slightly.

"Andrew's working in the back yard," he said. "Let me go and have a chat with him."

I heard some muffled voices—it seemed a few sharp words were being exchanged—and soon enough Wilson Jr. emerged. A taller, slimmer version of his father, he sported baggy jeans and a tool belt laden with wrenches and spanners. He leaned against the wall and stared at me blankly.

"I don't know anything," he said.

"Andrew . . . ," admonished his father.

"I don't . . . know . . . anything," he repeated. "Now, can I get back to work, please?"

"Listen," I said. "As I've just told your father, no one's in trouble here. I just want to know if you've been in contact with some people I'm looking for."

He stared at his hobnail boots and shook his head.

"I'm not the police, okay? I'm a pet detective. I find

missing animals. I'm working with a family who've had their beautiful little puppy stolen and who are absolutely bloody traumatized."

The boy briefly caught my gaze, before hurriedly looking away.

"All you need to do is to give them a call. To tell them that I'm on their case, and that, one way or another, I will find out what happened to Buffy."

Silence.

"And, if she is still alive, they need to either get in touch with me, or hand her in to a rescue center."

"Andrew . . . ," repeated his father, more sternly.

"All right, all right," he said, throwing up his hands in exasperation. "So, they rang me to get their wheels changed. I didn't want their business. They're wrong 'uns. They're trouble. But they said they were going to pay me a daft amount of money. Couldn't refuse it in the end, could I?"

"So you've got their contact details, then?" I asked. "And you can ask them about the missing dog?"

Andrew didn't answer for a long time. He was stalling and I was ready for his answer.

"My phone's broken," he said unconvincingly. "I dropped it. Smashed it to bits. I can't get their number. Sorry."

"That's no problem." I smiled. "I've got software that can retrieve data from a broken handset. Either that, or I could ask a contact of mine to access your phone records."

He gulped hard—his Adam's apple protruded like a peach stone—before glancing at his father. I'd forced him into a corner, and he knew it.

"Make that call, Andrew, and make it today," I said, patting Molly, who went from sitting to standing. "Just do the right thing. Please."

Two days later, Molly and I were traveling home from an afternoon spent trying to find a rare sphynx cat named Andromeda, when I got up a voicemail from Renu. Her squeals were so loud I had to turn down

Buffy at time of recovery

the volume on my speakerphone. "BUFFY'S BEEN FOUND!" she yelled, and a thunderbolt of adrenaline shot around my body. "Two young lads handed her in to a dog-rescue center in Essex," she panted, barely able to get her words out. "The staff scanned Buffy's microchip and rang me. Sachin and I are on our way. Never thought this day would happen. Never thought I'd see her again. Thank you so much, Colin. *Thank you SO, SO much . . .*"

There then followed a few seconds of joyful sobbing—I welled up, too, I'm not ashamed to admit—before the message clicked off. I looked in my rearview mirror and could see that Molly was shifting in her crate, seeking a comfortable sleeping position for the journey home.

"Well, well, well, Detective Constable Molly Butcher," I said, smiling. "Looks like we finally cracked our case."

I let out a deep sigh of relief. It had been a tough investigation, but Molly and I had solved it.

As soon as I got back to Cranleigh I called the rescue-center manager to learn more information about Buffy's return. He told me that two teenage boys had brought in the dog, and had left without saying a word. *Intermediaries*, I thought to myself. They had probably stepped in for the actual criminals, who certainly wouldn't have wanted their faces caught on security cameras, and who'd clearly wished to wash their hands of the dog they'd stolen. I'd made Buffy such a well-known figure in their area that she'd become too hot to handle.

I left Renu and her loved ones alone for a few days—I felt it was important that they were given plenty of time and space with Buffy—but we kept in touch via text and email. The puppy had received a clean bill of health from the vet's, she told me, and had been washed, groomed and pampered for the first time in four long months.

I paid a visit to them the following week. Watching Harry and Freddie running around the garden with their happy, healthy and fluffy little pooch was a sight to behold, and again reminded me of my brother David and I larking about with our canine friends in Singapore. I turned to Renu, who flashed me the most beautiful of smiles.

"I'll never forget what you've done for us, Colin," she said. "Our family is complete again."

"I couldn't have done it without Molly," I said, feeling a little overcome with emotion myself. I gave Renu a big hug before waving goodbye to the boys.

As I put Molly back into her crate, she gently nudged my arm and looked at me with concern, as if to say, *Are you all right, Dad? Your eyes look a bit sad . . .*

I was, I admit, mentally exhausted. The Buffy

investigation had taken several months to complete and I'd had to step up to the plate and show strength and confidence, even if, like Renu, I'd had my doubts about the outcome. Thank goodness I'd delivered on my promise, and Buffy was back where she belonged.

I looked down at Molly, who still seemed a little confused by my demeanor.

"I'm good, Molls, honestly," I said, ruffling the backs of her ears and kissing her snout.

10

BLUEBELL WOOD

Although Molly's scent-detection skills were coming on in leaps and bounds—quite literally, in fact—it was still vitally important that we kept up our rigorous training schedule.

There were always new techniques to learn and new hidey-holes to discover, and three or four times a week I'd take her over to Bramble Hill Farm in order to put her through her paces. Molly could often sense that we were off to HQ, and as I got everything ready at home she'd take up a position by the front door, usually sitting on my outdoor boots. As I pulled them onto my feet, she'd always gently place a paw on the leather, just making double-sure that we were venturing outdoors.

Sometimes I'd set Molly specific tasks at Bramble Hill, often based upon issues we'd encountered in previous searches. I would, for example, plant a cat-hair sample high up in a sycamore tree, to replicate the missing cat she'd found holed up in a treehouse. Or I'd take her to areas where small animals roamed—beside the lake, or along the canal—to teach her to focus on the core cat scent rather than being distracted by the odors of ducks, rabbits or squirrels.

While Molly's progress over the past few months had been nothing short of phenomenal, it was vital that her scent-detection techniques as a working cocker spaniel—as well as my own dog-handling abilities—were constantly improved and refined. This very fact had been underlined by Mark, the canine-behavior expert who'd worked so closely with Molly before she came home with me full-time.

"You'll never, ever stop improving, Colin," he'd told me on handover day. "Every single search will throw up different tests and challenges, and you've got to learn from them all, even the disappointments."

Indeed, Molly and I had experienced a handful of unsuccessful cat searches that spring. In one such instance I had unwisely deployed her in fine rain and, despite her very best efforts, it had been impossible for her to match the animal's scent in the damp conditions. The search was ultimately fruitless and, not only did I get soaked to the skin (as did Molly), I came away feeling utterly dejected. On another occasion we'd been tasked with finding a farm cat named Spider, but upon arrival at the location, I discovered that all the barns and stables were packed with livestock. Unable to guarantee Molly's safety, we'd had to leave without searching a single building.

I wasn't deluded—realistically, we were never going to locate every single cat—but I still felt down and disappointed whenever we didn't get a result, even if it was beyond our control. I would use these setbacks as a platform for further learning, however, and would put in hours of extra training to compensate.

"We'll get it right next time, Molls," I'd say as she tore off toward a cat-hair sample I'd hidden an hour earlier in a hollow oak tree.

On one such training day—a breezy springtime morning—I was driving over to Bramble Hill Farm while an impatient Molly bounced and bobbed around her crate.

C'mon, then, Dad . . . she seemed to be saying, as eager as ever to have some fun and fill her lungs with fresh air. *Are we nearly there yet?*

Then my phone rang, so I pulled over and took the call.

"Hello, Colin Butcher speaking . . ."

There followed a pause and then the sound of muffled voices, as if the phone receiver was being passed from one person to another.

"Good morning, dear," replied a frail, elderly voice. "Are you the pet detective?"

"Yes, that's me."

"The gentleman with the dog that finds cats?"

"Indeed." I smiled, and Molly whined petulantly behind me.

"I'm afraid I may need your help. I've heard all about you and Molly, and my kind colleagues here at the cat charity have found your telephone number. It's my Chester, you see. He's gone missing."

The lady's name was Margaret, she lived near the village of Hawkenbury and she'd had neither sight nor sound of her cat for three long days. An eighteen-year-old tabby, Chester was largely housebound and his extended absence was hugely out of character.

"I've been worried sick," she said. "He's not getting any younger and I'm petrified that he's come to some harm."

She explained that she and her sister—both in their mid-nineties—were unable to search their large garden and that numerous attempts by local villagers to find Chester had been unsuccessful.

"I simply can't bear it," she said, her voice faltering. "All I want is for my cat to be found, Mr. Butcher, and for me to know exactly what's happened to him. I don't suppose you and Molly could possibly help?"

"Firstly, you must call me Colin," I replied soothingly, "and, secondly, I'm sure that we can assist in some way. Ask one of your friends to text me your address and we'll be with you as soon as we can."

"Oh, that would be wonderful," she replied, sighing with relief. "That's just what I needed to hear."

I ended the call and turned to face my restless dog, who by now was emitting low growls of frustration.

"Change of plan, Molls. Training's abandoned. We're off to find Chester."

I picked up my trusty assistant along the way (Sam had become accustomed to last-minute plans for hasty assignments) and, following a scenic drive through the Surrey Hills, we reached Margaret's village around noon. We'd had a fair bit of trouble locating our client's home—we found ourselves in a maze of narrow, blossom-laden lanes, with a dearth of addresses—and it was only when we spied a tiny old lady leaning on a rickety wooden gate, squinting at the car, that we realized we'd reached our destination. As we pulled up, she waved cheerily, unlatched the gate and gestured toward a long, snaking driveway.

I slowly rolled down my window, noticing a rotting address sign on the ground. It was no wonder we'd had problems finding the place.

"Margaret?"

"Indeed it is. I'm so delighted to see you all," she said as Molly yapped excitedly and thumped her tail against her crate. My dog was smart enough to realize that the sound of a stranger's voice usually indicated that a live search was imminent.

Peering through my windshield, I spied a distant rooftop through a canopy of laurels.

"How's about hopping in the back seat, Margaret?" I asked. "Looks like a fair old trek to your front door."

"I'm fine, thanks," she replied. "The walk will do me good. Old dears like me need all the exercise they can get."

Fifteen minutes later Sam and I were leaning against my open trunk with the warm sun beating down on us, waiting for Margaret to emerge. Sitting between us, still in her crate, was an increasingly animated Molly. In these scenarios she would often tremble in anticipation, like she was shivering with cold, and would produce strange gargling noises from the back of her throat.

Come on, you two, my dog appeared to be saying. *Let's see some action . . .*

Facing us was Greenlea Hall, an imposing but dilap-idated Edwardian mansion. The grandeur of its sash windows, its lofty gables and its white portico was somewhat diminished, I noticed, by flaking paintwork and crumbling masonry. Parts of the coppery-red brickwork had been dislodged by a gnarled and knotty wisteria vine and at the front of the house stood a huge stone fountain, riven with cracks and covered in lichen.

Finally, Margaret hobbled into view. Her long, silvery-white hair was tied into a loose ponytail and she wore navy cotton trousers teamed with a baggy sky-blue sweater.

"So let me have a look at Molly." She grinned, stooping low and peering through the grate. "Oh, what a *gorgeous* girl. And a very, very clever doggy, from what I've heard . . ."

Molly's gurgles and tail thwacks promptly went into overdrive. "Oh, she'll love you for saying that," I laughed. "Flattery will get you everywhere with this little madam."

Margaret chuckled as she slowly straightened herself up. "So can I tempt you indoors for some tea and cake?"

I explained to Margaret that, while Sam and I would appreciate some refreshments, Molly would have to remain in the car until the start of the search. We had to be very careful not to expose her to any cat scent in the house; it might overwhelm her nostrils and hamper the search.

"I'll keep the trunk open for some fresh air, though, and I'll leave a couple of soft toys for her to gnaw. She'll be happy enough."

"Whatever's for the best." Margaret smiled, then ushered us toward her grand abode.

As we sat in her farmhouse kitchen—a room that had probably remained unchanged for decades—I gave my client a brief version of Molly's story. At the far end of the kitchen, near a huge, old stove, sat two other cats, a sleek Abyssinian and a scruffy Maine coon. Both were feigning a casual indifference, but I could tell by the odd flick of a tail and the twitch of an ear that they were more than aware of our presence.

"That's Simba and Sandy," said Margaret, gazing fondly at them, "although I have to say, they've not been themselves recently. They're both missing old Chester as much as I am."

All three cats had been strays, apparently, and were among the many lost or abandoned cats that Margaret had sheltered and adopted over the years. Animal aficionados like this lady were my favorite type of client, it has to be said: kind, compassionate and utterly devoted to their pets.

Suddenly, the mahogany kitchen door swung open, causing Sandy and Simba to leap up in fright and shoot out of the cat flap.

"Did I hear her saying she adopts them?" guffawed a gray-haired lady, clad in beige nylon slacks and an olive-green fleece. "What nonsense. My sister steals the things from our neighbors. She can't help herself. Loves those wretched cats more than she loves me."

"Oh, for goodness' sake, Kathrine," said Margaret, wearily shaking her head. "Colin, you've probably gathered that this is my sister. Please don't believe a word she says."

"Ah, so you're this detective fellow, are you?" she smirked, shuffling over and extending her bony hand. "Well, I hope you're not expecting to be paid, old chap," she continued, "because we haven't got a bean until the day I decide to sell this place. Not a bean."

"Kathrine!" cried her horrified sister.

"As it happens, I'm classing this visit as a training session for Molly," I responded, trying to stay measured. "I'm just happy to help your sister, to be honest."

"You'll probably be wasting your time, anyway," she harrumphed. "That animal's so decrepit it's probably dropped dead. Either that, or it's been flattened by a passing truck."

Margaret gasped and raised her hands to her flushed cheeks. *What a charmer*, I thought. *What an absolute charmer.* Sensing my mounting ire, Sam made a timely interjection.

"Colin, isn't it time for you and Margaret to go outside for the pre-search reconnaissance?" she said.

Sam knew that I always liked to have a safety-first sweep of the area beforehand, in order to identify any hazards that might endanger Molly's search: derelict outbuildings, rusty machinery or loose-lidded chemicals could be perilous.

". . . and while you do that, I can stay inside with Kathrine," she added with a wry smile. She had figured out, quite rightly, that I didn't want this overbearing sister sticking her nose in.

"Excellent idea," I replied.

Greenlea Hall, it transpired, was set in one of the largest estates in East Kent. Comprising a huge patchwork of lawns, fields and woodland, it also contained a smattering of dilapidated outbuildings and disused farm vehicles. Had Chester been a young, agile and independent cat, Molly and I would have definitely had our work cut out for us. But, in these circumstances, I didn't think a widespread search of the area would be necessary. My knowledge and experience of cat behavior told me that, taking into account his age, his frailty and his strong homing instinct, Chester would be found nearer rather than farther, and sooner rather than later.

"All things considered, Margaret, I'm pretty sure that Chester won't have strayed far," I told her.

"Oh, I do hope you're right," she replied. "Shall I show you around the gardens?"

Spanning the rear of Greenlea Hall was an impressive

glass orangery which bordered onto a huge, moss-covered stone terrace dotted with assorted buckets, plant pots and watering cans. This opened up onto an extensive lawn—a quarter the size of a soccer field, I reckoned—beyond which lay stunning views across the county. To the right was an empty paddock (Margaret had been an avid horsewoman back in the day, she told me) and to the left was a traditional walled garden. It, too, had seen better days, judging by its gangly fruit trees and scraggy herbaceous borders. An unkempt patch of grass was studded with daisies and dandelions and edged by a row of bare-branched oaks on one side and a line of bushy, overgrown firs on the other. In its prime, this garden would have been a hide-and-seek paradise for a curious child or a serene sanctuary for a frazzled parent. Those days were long gone.

"Chester used to love watching the world go by in here," said Margaret, her eyes glistening with tears. "He'd loll around in the sunshine and watch the blue birds flitting about. He was far too slow and tubby to catch any, of course."

I asked if I could take a peek inside the ramshackle garage, which housed the couple's vintage Mini Cooper, as well as a stack of antiquated gardening tools. As I shifted a pair of medieval hedge clippers to one side, I spied a cluster of rusty bicycles, in size order, ranging from a toddler's trike to a teenager's racer.

"They all belonged to my daughter," said Margaret wistfully. "I don't like to throw anything away. I . . . well . . . I thought they might be needed one day."

She explained that Greenlea Hall had belonged to her parents and that she and her sister had inherited it some thirty years ago. "My sister can be very outspoken," she said.

"Elizabeth lives in Cornwall now. She'll only visit when it's just me in the house, which—with Kathrine's arthritis—is hardly ever these days," she said. "We speak, and we write, but it's not the same. I feel like a stranger to my daughter. It's ever so sad."

Once upon a time, a great deal of love and labor must have gone into Margaret and Kathrine's dream family home. Now, sadly, it seemed that the place—and their friendship—had become run-down. I felt a sudden pang of sorrow for this delightful woman who, in her twilight years, seemed to be reaping most of her happiness from her pets, not her sibling.

"It's time for Operation Cat Sample," I said, smiling, and offered Margaret my arm for support as we strolled back toward the house. "And it's time to fetch the lovely Molly."

I remained on the terrace while Margaret retrieved Chester's favorite cushion, which, as instructed, she had kept away from Simba and Sandy and had left inside the house. Unfortunately, it was commonplace for cat owners to put their missing cat's bedding, favorite toy or litter tray outside in the garden in the mistaken belief this would encourage their cat to return. Sadly, this often attracted visits from other neighborhood cats, who would scent-mark these items, presenting the absent cat with yet another reason to stay away.

My heart leaped when my client appeared on the terrace with a large cushion balanced on her palms. At first I assumed it was made of mohair but, on closer inspection, I realized it was completely swathed in Chester's wispy beige fur. I felt like punching the air.

"I'm one of the few people in Britain who gets giddy when they see something covered in cat hair, Margaret," I grinned, thrilled that Molly now had the best possible chance of matching the scent and finding the pet.

Wearing latex gloves to ensure I didn't contaminate the sample with my own scent, I gently eased away several large clumps with a stainless-steel wire brush before carefully placing them into one of my sterile jam jars. Then, with everything good to go, I radioed Sam on the walkie-talkie to bring Molly across to the terrace. As usual, my dog was overjoyed to be reunited with me and gave my face a good old lick, with a dabbing of wet nose for good measure.

"It's search time, Molls," I said, looking into her eyes and stroking her sleek black head.

With a handful of dog treats in one pocket and my radio in the other, I led Molly over to the paddock to introduce her to Chester's scent. As professional as ever, she'd already composed herself accordingly and had entered a Zen-like state of calm and concentration. As her owner and handler, I'd taught her to differentiate between her two distinct roles—her life as a pet and her life as a worker—and she was able to make the transition from Molly the cuddly cocker spaniel to Molly the cat-seeking detection dog. The moment I took her harness from my belt and presented it to her she knew full well she was in work mode.

Responding to my usual "Toma" command, she poked her nose into the glass jar and inhaled deeply. On the command of "Seek . . . seek!"—and with Margaret and Sam now by my side—I finally let her off the leash and released her into a fairly stiff spring breeze.

With a shrill yelp of excitement, Molly shot across the wide lawn like a missile and, within a few seconds, appeared to hit a scent trail. Her snout seemed to stop while the rest of her body hurtled on—like something out of a Scooby-Doo cartoon—and she made a sudden ninety-degree swerve to the left, toward the walled garden. Through the gate she zoomed and, once we'd caught up with her, we watched as she crouched low, leaped high and gyrated around, inhaling the swirling air as she went.

However, it was when Molly zoned in on one of the largest conifers on the plot's eastern side that her behavior took a bizarre turn. Each time she took two steps forward she seemed to take one step back, all the while shooting us concerned glances. During our many searches together we had fostered a really unique understanding that often relied on eye contact and—knowing Molly as I did—I could immediately see that she had hit a scent that she'd never encountered before. As she circled the conifer, looking thoroughly dazed and disorientated, I could read her mind.

What's going on here, Dad? Why have I never smelled this before?

This erratic back and forth continued for a few minutes and my concerns began to mount. I had rarely observed her behaving like this. My dog was becoming increasingly distressed and confused and her anxiety levels were soaring. Something was really bothering her.

"I'm going to call her off for a while," I said to Margaret and Sam before recalling Molly with three pips of my dog whistle, the customary command that required her to pause the search and scamper back to my side.

"Don't worry, Molly," I said, comforting her with

pats and hugs before letting her frolic around a field for a few minutes. Only when I sensed that her agitation had receded and I was happy that our mutual trust remained intact did I decide to restart the search.

I reintroduced Chester's scent to my dog and, as I did so, I felt the headwind noticeably dropping. Yet again, Molly darted into the walled garden and ran toward the same fir, but this time she moved with a little more confidence and self-assurance. With bated breath, we all watched her as she crawled deep beneath the tree's heavy, grass-skimming branches.

Within seconds, Molly had dramatically reemerged and had suddenly performed the "down," lying flat, still and silent, with her front paws outstretched, her head upright and her eyes locked. Her unique success signal.

I've found what I'm looking for, she was effectively telling me.

I've done what you've asked . . .

This most emphatic and conclusive of "downs" told me that Molly had discovered Chester's scent and had pinpointed the lost pet. But her doleful expression, together with her strangely subdued demeanor, also spoke volumes. Margaret's cat was no longer alive.

I slowly knelt down on the grass and lifted the weighty branches. Sadly, my suspicions were confirmed. Lying on his side with his eyes closed, looking like he'd fallen into a deep, peaceful sleep, was a plump tabby cat. I could only surmise that poor Chester had succumbed to old age and had most likely passed away calmly and quietly after migrating to his little sanctuary.

"Bless you, Chester," I whispered, stroking his head before gently lowering the bough.

Then Margaret shuffled toward me, her hands clasped to her chest.

"Oh, Colin . . . has Molly found him? Is my Chester all right?"

I held her cold, fragile hands in mine as Sam looked on sadly. "I'm afraid it's not the news you were hoping for, Margaret," I said. "I'm ever so sorry."

After I walked a minute or so with Margaret, Sam gently took Margaret to one side. While I understood my client's pain, my focus had to be on my dog, who was both my priority and my responsibility. Out of the corner of my eye, I'd already seen Molly becoming increasingly anxious; she'd clearly picked up on Margaret's shock and my solemnity and, having never located a deceased pet before, was hugely perplexed by these negative post-search reactions. As far as she was concerned, she'd done her job as requested—at just shy of ten minutes, it had been her fastest ever cat recovery—yet, in her eyes, everyone must have seemed so unhappy. My dog, like many others, was remarkably sensitive to human emotion and it must have felt bewildering to witness such deep pain and suffering.

Compounding Molly's confusion was the absence of the usual reward experience, which—in these somber circumstances—would have been highly inappropriate and might have caused great offense to the client. I knew I had to give her the "Good girl, Molly!" treatment as soon as possible, though, since it was vital that Molly didn't associate the new scent as a negative experience but saw it as a positive. Failure to do so would mean that, next time she smelled a decaying cat, she might not indicate it for fear of upsetting me or a client.

With this in mind, I walked Molly over to the paddock, out of sight and sound of the grieving Margaret. Once inside, I rewarded her with gusto, I bombarded her with praise and laid on a quality play session.

Now this is what I call fun, she no doubt thought as she scampered after a tennis ball, deftly catching it in her mouth.

I found it a struggle to feign an upbeat cheeriness, to be honest. As an animal-lover myself, and as someone who'd mourned the loss of some beloved pets and people, Chester's death had greatly affected me, too. I felt dreadfully sorry for Margaret, but out of duty to Molly—and to preserve our regular routine—I felt obliged, as the old adage goes, to "keep calm and carry on." I remained in the paddock with Molly until I was satisfied that she'd been amply rewarded, and until I'd reinforced the fact that she hadn't been punished in any way, shape or form.

(Incidentally, this calculated decision, tough though it was, was vindicated a few weeks later when Molly found a missing cat that had sadly died after a suspected dog mauling. While the outcome was tragic, the owner was incredibly grateful to Molly and me for giving her closure to what had been a deeply upsetting experience. My dog, much to my relief, had not allowed the scent of decay to distract or distress her and so was still able to perform a successful scent match.)

On the way back from Greenlea Hall, Sam and I stopped off at a tiny rural café for a coffee. While Molly snoozed contentedly at our feet, emitting occasional snorts and snuffles, we took the opportunity to reflect upon an eventful afternoon.

"Thinking about it, Sam, I can see why Molly was so confused at the start of the search," I said, taking a frothy sip of cappuccino. "That smell of decay being blown around the garden distracted her. She'd never experienced that before."

Only when the wind had subsided, enabling the cat odor to settle and become more confined, had Molly had the conviction to isolate its location and finally find Chester.

Our conversation then moved on to the delightful Margaret, who'd clearly required our presence that day to provide her with much-needed comfort and closure.

"She needed that peace of mind, didn't she?" said Sam.

"She certainly did," I replied. "And thanks to Molly, she got it."

Upon hearing her name, my beloved dog slowly raised her head and stared into my eyes.

"You did a marvelous job, sweetheart," I said tenderly, giving her nape a little squeeze.

I'm pretty sure that Molly gave me the slightest of nods before dropping her head onto her paws and falling back to sleep.

11

THE DOG AND THE ADDER

Midsummer came and went and Molly and I reached a significant milestone. We had been together as a team for six whole months, our eventful journey having taken us from the training fields of Medical Detection Dogs to the verdant meadows of Bramble Hill Farm. Ever since that online advertisement had brought us together, Molly and I had developed an unbreakable bond and had shared some wonderful experiences. I had grown to love my little girl with all my heart—she was my companion as much as my colleague—and I simply couldn't imagine my life without her.

"Happy half-year anniversary, sweetheart," I'd said on the morning itself, presenting her with a box of multicolored tennis balls to celebrate the fact.

Sarah had watched, highly amused. "If memory serves, you didn't get me anything for putting up with you for six months," she said, with mock displeasure. "It's a good job I'm not the jealous type, eh?"

Then Sarah smiled at my dog, a really sweet, heart-felt smile; I'd never witnessed her display affection like this toward Molly before. For me, this was a watershed moment. It had taken a while—a very long while—but finally my girlfriend had fallen head over heels in love with Molly.

That lunchtime the three of us visited the Horse Guards Inn, a quaint, dog-friendly place nestled in the lovely South Downs National Park. I remember sitting at the table with my beloved partner by my side and my beautiful dog at my feet and almost pinching myself to check that I wasn't dreaming. I hadn't felt so happy in a long time. Life couldn't get much better than this, I reckoned.

I was blissfully unaware of the heartache that lay around the corner.

⁓

The following Wednesday, I awoke Molly at 5 a.m. in readiness for our latest cat search in the town of Amesbury. There was a valid reason for this ridiculously early start. The south of England was in the midst of a heatwave and I wanted to wrap up proceedings by midday in order to avoid the afternoon heat.

This particular case involved a missing cat named Cleo—a skittish, honey-colored Abyssinian—whose owner, Isobel, was an executive officer with the civil service. Her husband was a freelance cameraman, currently on an assignment in South Africa—and she'd recently returned to work following a one-year career break. She had not lived in Amesbury for long, she told me; earlier that year, the entire civil service had relocated to the town and Isobel's family had been among the first to take occupancy of one of the brand-new properties on a vast housing estate. Before its clearance, the site—much of it woodland—had been used by the Ministry of Defense for operations and maneuvers.

In the wake of Cleo going suddenly AWOL, and with work and house-moving commitments preventing her from organizing her own search, Isobel had requested my services as a matter of urgency. She explained that she'd also been thwarted by the lack of internet connectivity in her new home—she was unable to post appeals on social media—and, with the estate barely occupied, there were few neighbors around to spread the word or display posters. Reading about one of my successful recoveries in a local newspaper had prompted her to pick up the phone.

"I'm wondering if you and Molly could possibly come tomorrow?" she'd asked. "I could try and get the day off work. I know it's short notice, but I'd be ever so grateful. I just feel that Molly is my last chance of finding my cat."

Despite having my reservations—primarily weather-associated—I agreed to lend my assistance. This young lady clearly had a lot to cope with; the recent house move and return to work were taking up all her spare time, and—to compound matters—she had lost her pet cat. I felt dreadfully sorry for her.

There were, however, a few caveats. Mindful of the blisteringly hot conditions, I insisted on the search starting early. In addition, I'd not be expecting Molly to work past lunchtime—four hours a day was the cutoff point during the summer months, six hours when it was cooler—and she'd be doing so in twenty-minute shifts, with regular rest and refreshment breaks. And finally, if the temperature exceeded a certain level, I'd have no option but to bring the hunt for Cleo to a halt.

"I totally understand," said Isobel. "See you both tomorrow."

With the roads blissfully traffic-free, I arrived in Amesbury just after 7 a.m. I took the opportunity to have a quick drive around Isobel's community, just so I could get a decent understanding of its layout and geography. With fewer than a quarter of the red-brick properties occupied, it looked like something out of a film set, and—with a dearth of trees and hedges—it had an eerie, soulless quality. A narrow strip of woodland—about 100 yards wide and 500 yards long—split the estate from a busy divided highway, down which cars, motorbikes and trucks hurtled at great speed.

I hope Cleo hasn't tried to cross that road, I thought to myself. *She wouldn't have lasted long if she had . . .*

Molly and I made our way to Isobel's home and were greeted in the doorway by a tall woman with a sandy-colored pixie cut. I declined her kind offer of a coffee and a croissant—I wanted to get to work immediately—and, once Molly was exposed to a sample of Cleo's scent, the three of us began an exhaustive (and exhausting) search of the estate. We visited the occupied households first, wherein most neighbors were breakfasting or readying themselves for work; they were happy to let us explore their gardens and garages. We found no trace of the cat, unfortunately, so we switched our focus to the uninhabited properties. Molly checked front gardens and back lawns for scent trails, while Isobel and I peered through living room windows and patio doors, just in case she'd crept in while building work was taking place. It was all to no avail, sadly.

As the mid-morning temperatures soared, the scarcity of shade became a problem. I found myself constantly stopping to give Molly a break—she was panting quite heavily—and I watched with concern as she thirstily slurped pint upon pint of fresh water. I began to get a bad feeling about the whole endeavor and started to wish I'd never agreed to pursue it in the first place.

You really shouldn't work Molly in these conditions, Colin, heckled a voice in my head. *It's not very fair on her, is it?*

However, having committed to the search, and out of duty to my careworn client, I felt obliged to continue. Working as a pet detective, I found myself dealing with some very anguished clients and, for that reason, my empathy and sympathy had a habit of clouding my judgment.

My decision to persist with the search for Cleo was one that I'd come to regret deeply.

~ ~ ~ ~ ~

At the three-hour mark, as midday approached, I decided to investigate the wooded area nestled between the road and the estate. I hoped that its canopy of trees and the dappled sunlight would make things cooler and more comfortable for Molly.

"There's a good chance that Cleo came here to explore," I told Isobel, "so let's see if Molly can find any scent."

I gave her totally free rein, without any guidance or

direction from me ("working her nose," I called it) and observed her closely as she snuffled around shrubs and brambles at head height and grass and bracken at ground level. Within a few minutes, she appeared to detect a strong odor, whirling around and contorting her body as the scent infiltrated her nostrils. With Isobel and me following in her wake, she dashed toward a bowl-shaped dip in the ground before skidding to a sudden halt. There, much to our surprise, was a tiny fawn, no more than a few days old, trembling with fear at the sight of two perplexed humans and a puzzled dog.

"Awww, poor little mite," whispered Isobel.

"Its mother probably bolted when she heard us approaching," I replied. "She'll be back soon, I'm sure."

Other than being in panic mode, the gangly little creature seemed healthy and well—I gently checked it over for injury—so we left it there, to be reunited with its parent.

The new sights, smells and sounds of the woodland had clearly heightened Molly's senses, and moments later she was charging off in pursuit of a second scent.

Molly closed in on a fallen, rotten tree trunk, while Isobel peered over my shoulder. Behind the tree lay the source of my dog's erratic behavior: a large and lifeless badger that had most likely been hit by a vehicle on the highway before staggering to its final resting place.

"Oh, that's awful," said Isobel, averting her eyes, as a couple of hungry crows circled above the carcass.

I felt a pang of sadness, not only for the unfortunate badger, but also for its fellow wildlife. The recent construction of the car-clogged road and the housing community had not only compromised their safety and seclusion but had also greatly reduced the size of their natural habitat. Years before, they'd been able to roam for miles, but now they were confined to this tiny strip of land.

It was at that point that my phone alarm beeped, reminding me that the search for Cleo had reached the four-hour mark and—for Molly's sake (she was becoming increasingly hot and bothered)—it was time to wrap everything up. In a perfect world, we'd have found the missing cat but, sadly, it wasn't to be. Isobel looked crestfallen.

"Can we just check one more spot, Colin?" she begged tearfully. "It'll take half an hour, maximum, I promise . . ."

Against my better judgment—and undoubtedly swayed by my client's pleading eyes—I acquiesced and allowed Isobel to lead me to a nearby leafy glade. The ever-sensitive Molly seemed to understand this woman's despair and, as I released her from her leash, she somehow mustered up enough energy to break cover, galloping twenty yards ahead and zooming through a thicket of rhododendrons.

There came a point when I could hear the sound of Molly's tail thwacking against branches but could no longer see her in my line of vision. This was hugely remiss on my part; I'd been taught by Rob and Mark at MDD never to lose sight of her and never to let her stray too far ahead.

I tried desperately to catch up, ducking under low-hanging trees and dodging their crisscrossed roots. I eventually spotted Molly scampering up a yard-high mound of earth, her tail wagging, her nose snuffling, as if she'd detected yet another scent trail. From where I stood, this small dune of soil looked like the detritus from a fox den, which I'd encountered on many occasions in the countryside.

"She seems pretty excited about something . . . ," said a hopeful Isobel.

"Sadly, I don't think it's Cleo," I replied. While it wasn't unusual for cats to use these snug holes as hiding places once the foxes had departed, the absence of Molly's "down" signal suggested she hadn't found an odor match.

Then, just as I was about to recall her and bring the search to a close, Molly let out an ear-splitting, blood-curdling howl. She reared up on her back legs and fell backward, hitting the ground with an almighty thud.

"Molly . . . oh my god, *MOLLY*!" I yelled, sprinting over as fast as my legs could carry me.

I was confronted with the heart-stopping sight of my dog lying motionless on the ground, her breathing heavy and rapid, her eyes glazed and unseeing. My head was pounding but I tried to stay calm and invoke my first-aid skills, kneeling beside her to check for any blood on her body or for any sign of broken bones. All I found was a sticky, unguent substance near her throat area; it definitely wasn't blood, so I assumed it was some kind of tree sap. I also noticed a sharp, jagged stick on the ground, which led me to wonder whether she'd impaled herself in some way.

"Colin, what on *earth* has happened?" cried Isobel, rushing over to the fox earth.

"I don't know, but it's serious," I said, my voice shaking as I slowly, carefully, scooped up my dog's hot, trembling body. "I need to get her to a vet straightaway."

As we hurried back to my car, Molly began to hyperventilate—she emitted a weird, low moaning sound—and her eyes began to dilate alarmingly. Her body started to stiffen, too, as if it was going into paralysis. I quickly laid her on the grass and grabbed a bottle of water from the trunk, using half of it to douse her coat and drip-feeding the rest into her lolling, drooling mouth. Isobel was already sitting in my passenger seat, telling the local vet's office to expect the arrival of a very ill cocker spaniel.

It was then that I noticed a slight swelling on Molly's chest—near where the gluey substance had oozed—and it suddenly dawned on me what might have happened.

A snakebite . . . a venomous snakebite, I thought to myself as a chill ran down my spine. Adders were prevalent in the south of England, although, in my experience, their natural habitat tended to be open grassland and coastal areas rather than woodland.

As I lifted Molly into the car, she yowled in pain and sank her teeth into my right hand. It was a reflex response to the pain she must have been feeling and, despite being in abject agony, I let her stay clamped on until she finally relaxed her jaw and released her incisors. After gently laying my dog into her crate, I sped to the vet, using my police-driving skills to cut through the heavy traffic and parking on double yellow lines. This was an emergency in every sense.

I left Molly in the car with Isobel—I wanted her to be assessed properly before I moved her again—and dashed into the office. It was a tiny place, with only one vet on site.

"My dog's extremely ill," I panted. "I'm not exactly

sure what happened, but there's a chance it was a snakebite. She's in lots of pain, and she may be in paralysis. Can she be seen, please?"

The female receptionist looked up from her computer. "Are you registered with us?"

"Er, no, I'm not local, so . . ."

She slid a two-page form over to me and handed me a pen. "Can you fill this in first?"

I felt a sudden surge of anger.

"My dog is gravely ill. She could be dying."

I didn't make a habit of berating receptionists, but this was plain ridiculous.

"It's procedure, I'm afraid," she replied, with a nonchalance that further fueled my ire.

"I want my dog to be seen now, before it's too bloody late."

The vet, who'd been loudly ordering pharmaceuticals in his office, came out to see what was causing all the commotion. Through gritted teeth, I repeated my concerns, and—after nodding knowingly at his receptionist—he agreed to check Molly over.

"In fact, let me fetch a muzzle first," he said, eyeing the angry-looking bite marks on my hand.

Outside, I thanked Isobel for waiting with Molly and gave her ten pounds for a taxi home so she could collect her daughter. My client looked mortified that the search had ended so miserably.

"I'm so sorry this has happened, Colin," she said. "Do keep me informed."

"You, too," I replied. (I later learned that Cleo was never found. I presumed she'd met the same fate as the poor badger.)

As the vet and I carried a woozy and wheezy Molly from the car to the office, I noticed with horror that the swelling on her chest had almost tripled in size, to grapefruit-like proportions. I felt like screaming. My darling dog's life was in the balance and she seemed to be slipping away before my very eyes.

"It could well be a snakebite, but I can't be sure," said the vet, moving a stethoscope around Molly's body as she lay still on the treatment table. "We're only a satellite office, and I think she needs specialist care at our main clinic. I'll give her some painkillers for the time being, but I'd prefer it if my colleagues assessed her."

This wasn't what I wanted to hear. I'd hoped for immediate answers and treatment, and I was infuriated by the vet's apparent lack of urgency and the clinic's dearth of resources.

The receptionist called a veterinary ambulance and, within minutes, a white Range Rover arrived, sirens blaring, to whisk my poor Molly away. I planned to follow behind in my own car, once I'd filled out those precious forms.

I walked outside and collapsed onto a nearby bench.

I sat there for five minutes or so, my head in my hands, my stomach lurching, desperately trying to pull myself together before I made the journey. Consumed with guilt and remorse, I couldn't quite believe my own stupidity. I shouldn't have taken on the case. I shouldn't have worked Molly in that heat. I shouldn't have agreed to extend the search. And, more than anything, I shouldn't have put my client's needs before my dog's. With one hand, I'd offered a new life to the most adorable rescue puppy, and, with the other, I'd almost taken it away. I had let her down badly and I wasn't sure I could ever forgive myself. "My poor Molly," I whispered, swallowing hard as I pictured her alone and bewildered in the ambulance. "This is all my fault, sweetheart, and I'm ever so sorry . . ."

While I'd been wrapped up in my own thoughts, a silver-haired woman with soft blue eyes had quietly taken a seat beside me.

"Pardon me for intruding," she said, "and I won't be so rude as to ask what's upset you, but I just want to say that everything is going to be just fine and you don't need to worry."

"Thank you," I said to the old lady. "Thank you so much."

She patted my hand with maternal concern before going off on her way.

During the drive to the vet's main clinic I took the opportunity to phone Sarah at home, Sam in the office, and my son, Sam, in Manchester, as well as seeking the advice of my own vet, Graham.

"Yep, I reckon that sounds like a classic case of an adder bite," he said, having listened to a blow-by-blow account of the incident, together with a list of Molly's symptoms. He knew a lot about that species of snake, informing me that it wasn't that uncommon for adders to slither into woodland to hunt for lizards, voles and other small animals. After making their kill, these snakes would often rest in the shade to digest their food, so lazing on a fox earth, under some trees, sounded entirely plausible.

"Molly probably detected the adder's scent and took it by surprise," he explained. "It may well have been weighed down with food so wouldn't have been able to escape as quickly as it normally would. Its only option would have been to defend itself, hence the bite and the venom release."

"Graham, I only wish you'd been my first port of call," I told my vet of choice, explaining how underwhelmed I'd been with the clinic in Amesbury and how I didn't hold out much hope for their sister practice, where I was currently heading.

"Right, here's my advice, Colin," he said, with characteristic pragmatism. "My surgery's closed for the day, but I suggest you pick up Molly and take her to the animal Accident and Emergency unit here in Guildford. It'll be too late to administer anti-venom—that should have been done straightaway—but she'll get the best possible care. Bring her to my surgery first thing tomorrow morning and I can examine her thoroughly and give you a much clearer diagnosis."

That sounded like a plan—I had every faith in Graham—and within the hour I'd collected Molly. The good news, according to the veterinary nurse, was that her condition had remained stable during the journey and she'd maintained consciousness. As for the bad news, however, the swelling was still significant (despite the antibiotics that had been administered in the ambulance) and she was still desperately sick. The nurse totally understood my desire to bring Molly closer to home, though, and sent us on our way with her good wishes.

After a careful drive back to Guildford I dropped Molly off at the emergency animal clinic. There, specialist staff would monitor her around the clock and keep her as comfortable as possible. As a veterinary nurse prepared to wheel her down to the ward, I bade my beloved dog a heartfelt farewell. I kissed her shiny head, stroked her floppy ears and gazed into her glassy, rheumy eyes.

"Everything's going to be fine, Molls," I said, trying

to keep my tone and gestures as cheery and upbeat as possible so as to generate positive vibes. "Everyone's going to do all they can to make you better, I promise."

My dog let out a weary little whine as the nurse gently placed her on the trolley. I didn't wait to see her being trundled off down the corridor. I didn't want her to turn around and see her owner looking so worried and upset.

Unpacking all the search equipment from the car when I got back home was unbearable. On any normal day, Molly would have been snapping at my heels and tearing around the driveway, relishing the prospect of our customary post-search play session. But it had been anything but a normal day—it had been a nightmarish day, in fact—and as I placed her UK Pet Detectives harness into my bag I felt her absence deeply.

Sarah provided some much-needed comfort that evening, listening to my concerns and anxieties, assuring me that Molly was receiving excellent care and making me a soothing hot chocolate. It didn't have the desired effect, however, and I experienced a sleepless night. I couldn't stop thinking about the day's events—particularly my own accountability—and, not only that, my hand was still throbbing in pain (mercifully, I was up-to-date with my tetanus shot).

Unable to get any shut-eye, I ended up paying a

Molly and her inflamed chest after the snakebite

2 a.m. visit to my home office, feeling a deep pang of sadness when I padded past Molly's empty bed. I spent a couple of hours surfing the internet, researching all I could about adders and how they "envenomed" their prey. The more cases I studied, the more convinced I was that Molly had been one such victim. Reassuringly, in most of these snakebite incidents, the dogs had eventually pulled through. In a few hours' time I'd find out whether Molly would do the same.

I returned to the clinic at 6:30 a.m. and received the news that, while the swelling was still a major concern, Molly had slept peacefully and had responded well to medication. She was brought out by the on-call vet, looking very dazed and confused. I knelt down beside her, getting as close as I could so she could recognize my scent. My dog drowsily nuzzled into me, using what was left of her energy to give me a loving lick on the cheek. *Hey, Dad*, she seemed to be saying. *What's happening to me? Who are these strangers? Where have you been all night?*

The vet helped me lift her into her crate and we headed to our fourth veterinary practice in the space of twenty-four hours.

Graham took a good look at Molly as she lay meekly on his treatment bed. She still seemed very ill, he surmised, and would need a comprehensive examination—under general anesthetic—to check the extent of the bite and the impact of her fall.

"The chest swelling is definitely a reaction to the snake venom," he said, "but I also want to arrange an X-ray. I'm rather concerned that she might have sustained an injury when she fell back onto the ground. A fracture, perhaps, where the humerus meets the scapula."

"A fracture?"

"Yep, it's entirely feasible. And I feel obliged to tell you, Colin, if it happened to be a complex break, I probably wouldn't be able to operate."

Graham saw my horrified expression and placed a soothing hand on my shoulder.

"My advice to you, my friend, is to take yourself away for a couple of hours and let me attend to Molly.

Go and grab yourself some breakfast. There's no point you hanging around here; you'd only be pacing around the waiting room."

"You're probably right," I said, "but you must keep me updated."

"'Course I will, Colin." He smiled as Molly looked up at me with doleful eyes. "And please don't worry. She's in great hands."

In the Speckledy Hen Café, just around the corner from the vet's, I ate a full English breakfast, drank a gallon of coffee and answered a few texts from concerned relatives. All the café staff adored Molly and the look of shock on their faces when I explained her absence only compounded my feelings of guilt.

Just as the clock struck 10 a.m., Graham called.

"Molly's in recovery—she's doing okay, considering—so make your way over here and I'll tell you what I've found."

Graham had plenty to impart. He hadn't discovered any broken bones, thank heavens—so no surgery would be required—and, having shaved off the fur on Molly's chest to enable closer examination, it had become apparent that she'd been bitten by the adder not once, but twice.

"Let's just say that Molly's an extremely lucky dog, Colin," said Graham. "One of the puncture wounds missed her main carotid artery by fractions of an inch, so things could have been so much worse. Catastrophic, in fact."

If the venom had gone straight to her heart, he explained, she could have died almost instantly. But because it hit muscle tissue instead, the toxin was dispersed much more slowly, at a rate that a young, fit, healthy dog like Molly was able to survive. I let out a huge sigh of relief.

"But we still have to proceed with caution," said the vet. "While it's true to say that Molly has withstood the initial bite, she's certainly not out of the woods, and there remains a small chance that she won't make it."

"What do you mean?" I asked, my heart racing.

"I'll be straight with you," he replied. "Snake fangs contain all sorts of nasty bacteria, and I think there's a strong possibility that Molly will contract a secondary infection, which can occasionally prove to be fatal. But your dog's a tough little cookie, Colin, and I've every faith that she'll pull through."

"My god, Graham, I hope you're right . . ."

"So here's the plan. I'm going to let you take her home, but I'll be prescribing her a course of very strong antibiotics to try and fend off any infection. She'll also need plenty of fluid, and lots of rest."

Once Molly had fully slept off the anesthetic, I was able to drive her back home. I spoon-fed her some food, gave her a bath and lowered her into her favorite bed.

I then sat on the floor and talked her to sleep, just like I'd done with Sam when he was a baby. I regaled her with the story of how Molly the Clever Dog had found Rusty the Missing Cat in the summerhouse, reminding her how very, very proud she'd made me feel that day. I must have drifted off myself because, a few hours later, I felt Sarah gently shaking my shoulder.

"Come to bed, Colin," she whispered, as Molly snoozed soundly beside me. "She's nice and settled now, and you need a decent sleep, too."

Nursing Molly through those first few days was extremely tough. I kept a vigil by her bedside, attending to her every need and monitoring her every move (and mood) for signs of progress or deterioration. I totally shut myself off from work for a week—Sam and Stefan took over the reins, ensuring the smooth running of our ongoing investigations—and, to save time, I distributed group emails instead of answering individual messages. I had received hundreds of well-wishing calls from concerned friends, family and colleagues—including the Medical Detection Dogs team—and it was so heartening to think that everybody was rooting for us.

For the first twenty-four hours, Molly seemed to rally a little—she was able to move around her room, albeit slowly and gingerly—but on day two she took a serious turn for the worse. Her temperature rocketed, her energy levels plummeted and her breathing became shallow and labored. I went into panic mode, terrified that this was the perilous secondary infection that Graham had warned me about. I called him immediately, only for him to confirm my worst fears.

"She's clearly fighting off that infection, Colin. Keep up the antibiotics and fluids and make sure she stays cool and rested."

I did as he instructed and, for forty-eight hours, I barely left Molly's side. Gradually, she showed signs of improvement, and on the morning of day four, it was as if a magic recovery button had been pressed.

"What the heck . . . !" I gasped as a bright-eyed Molly bounded into my bedroom early that morning, jumping onto my bed and smothering me with kisses.

I'm back!!! she seemed to be saying. *Let's play!!!*

That same afternoon, I took Molly to the vet for a checkup. Mercifully, she was over the worst of the infection, but I was rather concerned about the pronounced limp she'd developed.

"You're right, there's a distinct lameness in her front-right paw," said Graham, examining her. "She's been overcompensating on her right-hand side, it seems, because the pain from the snakebite was more acute on the left."

He suggested that, in order to rectify the problem, I needed to book Molly onto a regimen of canine aqua therapy. If it went well, this non-weight-bearing exercise would reduce any feelings of pain or strain and would gradually build up her confidence.

"Eventually, she'll almost forget that she's lame," added Graham. "I wholeheartedly recommend it."

I took Graham's advice and reserved some sessions at a nearby specialist center. Molly looked unbearably cute in her life jacket, and it was so funny watching from the sidelines as she doggy-paddled around. The swim therapist—who was excellent—would gently push Molly to the center of the tank before letting her swim to the steps. Then, just as she reached her destination, the therapist would nudge her back to the middle again. All the while, Molly wore a perplexed *What the heck is going on?* expression as she was cast adrift, again and again.

Much to my delight, these sessions seemed to do the trick. Soon afterward we were able to resume our country walks and begin some light exercise but, strangely enough, Molly's limp occasionally reappeared when she was at home. It was Sarah, in fact, who tactfully suggested that my darling dog might be milking things a little.

"Colin, have you noticed that Molly only limps when

you're around, especially if she wants something from you?" she said as we both watched TV one evening.

"I'm not sure that's true," I replied, thinking my girl-friend was being a tad harsh.

"But she doesn't limp at all if you're not in the room. I was looking at her through a crack in the door this morning."

"I very much doubt that, honey . . ."

Sarah was misguided, I decided. Granted, Molly had received oodles of attention and affection from me during her illness and recovery, but surely she couldn't be so shameless. But my partner had aroused my curiosity, so much so that as an experiment, I rigged up one of my covert cameras in the living room.

Sarah and I couldn't stop laughing when I played back the footage.

"Molly, you little madam," I grinned, watching her feign a heavy limp in return for a fuss and a cuddle, then walking completely normally once I'd left the lounge. The mischievous Molly of old was back in the room, that was for sure.

While I'd tried not to think about Molly's capacity for work during her illness—her welfare as my pet had

been my prime concern—as her recovery continued, a few worrying questions began to swirl around
my head. Would she ever be able to work alongside
me again? Had the snakebite affected her scent-
recognition skills? Would she ever find another missing cat? And would this harrowing experience deter
her from searching woodlands?

It was time to have a frank conversation with Mark
Doggett regarding her future. Concerned that the
Amesbury incident might have dented both her confidence and her ability as a scent-detection dog, I needed
to know what was best for her well-being, whether it
was continuing with her work with me as normal, being
retrained from scratch at MDD, or spending the rest of
her life solely as my pet. Ending our work partnership
would surely break my heart—my little pal and I had
made such excellent progress together—but Molly's
welfare was paramount.

"The simple way to find out, Colin, is by setting up
a training exercise at Bramble Hill Farm," said Mark.
"No help, no promptings, no encouragement, just let
her work it out for herself. You'll soon know if she's still
up to the job."

So, on a cool August afternoon with a strong and
steady breeze, I organized a task for Molly, like I'd done
hundreds of times before. The cat-hair sample—which

I'd obtained from a friend's tabby kitten—was hidden among some long grass, in the middle of a two-acre field. I also wore my GoPro camera so I could email the footage back to Mark.

"Toma," I said, my heart thumping as Molly's snout filled the jam jar and took the scent. As usual, she let out one solitary bark, which always meant *Okay, Dad, I've got the scent memorized . . . let's get going . . .*

"Molly, seek, seek!" I commanded, sending her on her way with a flourish of my hand.

The moment of truth had arrived.

She seemed a little hesitant at first—I could definitely discern a very slight limp, too—but within half a minute she had begun to bound around the field, her tail wagging vigorously behind her. I watched nervously as she performed a series of swooping, swerving S-shapes, following the direction of the summer breeze as it dispersed an array of scent particles.

Gosh, I've missed this, Molly appeared to be saying, as if she'd suddenly remembered the freedom of the outdoors and the thrill of a search.

A smile spread across my face when, about two hundred yards ahead of me, my dog zoned in on the hidden sample and slammed her trembling body down beside it, giving me that familiar *Found it, Dad!* signal. I let out a deep sigh of relief.

Despite all that pain and trauma, Molly had clearly

lost none of her incredible skills. I gave her a click on my marking device—the signal to return for her reward—and she came hurtling back across the field, sporting a wide, pink-tongued doggy grin.

"Good girl, Molly," I said, clasping her close with one hand and feeding her treats with the other. "You, young lady, will never cease to amaze me . . ."

12

THE CAT AND THE RIVERBOAT

Although Molly and I were back in business, some serious lessons had been learned. In the wake of the snakebite incident I'd been forced to reassess my priorities and revise my procedures; from now on, no work-related matter would supersede Molly's health and well-being. Never again would I put her life in jeopardy by bowing down to a client's demands, however desperate the situation. My pre-search risk-assessment policy would be tightened, too, insofar as I'd simply decline to offer my assistance if Molly's safety couldn't be guaranteed. The hideous experience in Wiltshire had come as a stark reminder of my responsibilities to this precious little creature and I was determined not to lose sight of that fact.

One of our first post-illness assignments proved to be quite memorable, as it happened. I was contacted by a couple—Edward was an art dealer and Lily was a property surveyor—who had recently rented out their first-floor flat in London and bought an old houseboat. Their reasons were twofold: first, their busy lifestyles meant that they hardly spent any time together, and, second, Lily wanted to finish her master's degree in Bristol and needed to move closer to the university to complete her studies. The couple had hatched a plan to dock their boat on the nearby canal, so that Lily could attend her lectures and Edward could set about restoring the boat and also make the occasional commute into London. They would spend a leisurely few days sailing the houseboat down the River Thames until they reached Reading, at which point they'd lift the boat out of the water and have it transferred by a large truck to the Kennet and Avon Canal.

They wouldn't be alone on the deck, though. Traveling with them would be Sapphire, their beloved British Blue pedigree cat, who'd been part of their little family unit for years. While they were confident that their pet would love living on the houseboat once it reached its final destination, away from the hustle and bustle of London, they were also conscious that the journey might prove to be tricky. They had even considered asking Edward's father to drive Sapphire over to the Bristol marina, but not only did she suffer with car sickness, she hated being separated from her owners.

The trio began their maiden voyage along the river

early one summery morning. Little Sapphire remained in the cozy living quarters with either Edward or Lily (the couple took turns at the controls) and spent her time curled up asleep or peeking through the porthole windows, watching the world flow by.

As dusk set in, they moored for the night in the village of Hurley. They awoke very early in the morning— the cat had spent the whole night snuggled at the foot of their bed—and after a quick bowl of cereal (and a pouch of cat food for Sapphire) they continued on their journey.

Edward and Lily had been on the move for ten minutes when they realized, much to their horror, that the cat was missing. The couple were almost certain that she'd been with them when they'd left Hurley, and Lily recalled having seen her playing with one of the boat's fenders. However, after we conducted a frantic search both above- and belowdecks, she was nowhere to be found. They made a swift about-turn and headed back to the dock, where they spent the next few hours roaming the riverbank and beyond, repeatedly yelling, "*Sapphire* . . . ch-ch-ch . . . *Sapphire* . . . ch-ch-ch!" They were terrified that she'd fallen overboard and, in sheer desperation, searched for "pet detective" on their phone and gave me a call.

"Our cat's gone missing," Edward said, sounding utterly woebegone. "We think she's either jumped or fallen from a houseboat and may have drowned. Please, please, can you help us find her? It's getting dark and we're starting to panic."

"Firstly, you need to stay calm," I replied. "Secondly, you mustn't discount the fact that she's still alive. It's not beyond the realm of possibility that she's made it ashore."

"But how?" asked Edward. "Cats can't swim."

"Ah, now that's a common misconception," I explained, relieved to be able to offer him a crumb of comfort. I told him that most cats could, in fact, swim—hence the evolution of their slightly webbed feet—but they invariably choose not to. Some breeds, though—like Bengals—actively loved the water and were known to jump into the bath or shower with their owners. "That's reassuring to know," he replied, "but if it is the worst-case scenario and she's washed up on a riverbank, poor thing, I still need her to be found. She's like family to us, and Lily and I would want to give her a proper burial. The thought of her just drifting down the Thames, alone . . . well . . ." And that's when his voice finally cracked. "That would just break our hearts."

Eager to employ Molly's cat-detection skills, he asked if I could possibly bring my dog over to Berkshire, preferably the sooner the better. I agreed to pay him a visit the next morning—fortunately for him, my schedule was free for a couple of days—but I was at pains to stress the complex nature of this case, due principally to the enormity of the search area and the ambiguity of her disappearance. I also explained to Edward that, in order to maximize the chances of finding Sapphire, he'd need to provide me with some decent cat-hair samples.

"That shouldn't be a problem," he replied. "My dad's clearing out our flat in London at the moment and Sapphire had lots of sleeping spots there so I'm sure he won't mind bringing some of her stuff over."

"Excellent. Look forward to seeing you both in the morning, Edward. And do try and get some sleep."

It was my first ever visit to the village of Hurley, and as Molly and I enjoyed a walk around (and I performed a rigorous risk assessment), I was impressed with what I saw. Whitewashed, red-roofed houses lined the narrow roads and the charming little village comprised a quaint corner shop, an ancient abbey and two lovely country pubs. There was also a typically English cricket pitch and pavilion, beyond which lay a well-maintained RV park overlooking the River Thames.

Meeting me by the towpath, clutching a wad of MISSING CAT leaflets in one hand and a reporter's notebook in the other, was Edward's father, Godfrey. A tall, gray-haired retired teacher, he explained that his son had decided at the last minute to continue on to Bristol with Lily; she was reluctant to sail alone—understandably so—and Edward would be joining us later that day. It seemed Godfrey had spent most of the morning scouring the streets, engaging with villagers (he'd compiled copious notes in spidery handwriting) and distributing his hastily printed handouts.

"Delighted to be joining your team for the day, Mr. Butcher," he boomed in a deep voice, startling a couple of passing ducks, who hastily waddled off in the opposite direction. "You, me and Molly will crack this case, I'm sure of it."

Suppressing a wry smile, I outlined my plan to this self-appointed sleuth. I told him I was working on the optimistic theory that the cat was still alive and had either sneaked off the barge prior to setting sail the previous morning or had jumped or fallen off the deck while the barge was moving. I was holding on to the hope that she'd managed to swim ashore.

"Cats massively bond to their territory, Godfrey," I told him, "so it was probably very disorientating for Sapphire to be relocated from the flat to the houseboat. It would have been a shock to her system, and she perhaps instinctively headed back to dry land."

"Yes, that's exactly what I was thinking," he murmured, tapping his pencil against his crooked teeth. I couldn't quite work out whether this guy was going to be a help or a hindrance. Judging by the way she point-edly kept her distance, I don't think Molly was too sure of him either.

"First things first, Godfrey, have you brought the cat-hair samples?" I asked.

"Why, of course," he said, performing a mini-salute. "Follow me."

He led us to his bottle-green Volvo, where, on the back seat, lay a pile of Edward's clothing that had been collected from the flat. Nestled against it was a canvas bag full to the brim of Sapphire's toys, cushions and bedding, most of it covered in a thick layer of charcoal-gray cat hair. On the back seat was the biggest scratching post I'd ever seen.

"Took me bloody ages to get that thing in the car," said Godfrey.

I'm not surprised, I thought.

My heart sank slightly; this mix-up of items meant that I wouldn't be obtaining the purest of samples—usually, I'd extract them from the source myself, under sterile conditions—but, on this occasion, they'd just have to suffice. In any case, Molly was more than capable of isolating single odors from a mishmash of others and there was no reason she couldn't do this again. I wielded my trusty tweezers, carefully transferred a chunk of hair into a glass jar and sealed the lid nice and tightly.

As I headed toward the river, Godfrey suddenly

boomed, "Wrong way, matey!" He informed me that, during his own mini-search of the village that morning, he'd struck up a conversation with a local farmer who'd reported seeing a dark-colored cat enter one of his large barns.

"He let me have a quick look around the building," he said, nodding sagely, "and I think it could prove to be a rather promising lead. That's where I'd like to start the search, if that's okay with you."

This fellow's assertiveness was beginning to irritate me—I had to remind myself that I was working at the behest of the distraught owners—but I agreed to what he said and headed over to the farm. If it was a genuine sighting, it needed following up.

The barn in question wasn't used for farming purposes, it transpired, but rented out as a storage facility for local boat and barge owners. It housed crafts of all shapes and sizes, from single-berth speedboats to fifty-foot catamarans.

"Wow, this may take some time," I said to Godfrey, surveying this gigantic space and the plethora of potential hiding places.

I couldn't believe my eyes therefore when, within a minute of her snout snuffling the jam jar, Molly gave me a perfect "down" near the barn entrance. She flattened her body, outstretched her front paws and awaited her customary treat.

To my utter bewilderment, however, there was no trace of a cat. Godfrey and I searched high and low, corner to corner, but with zero results. There were none of the usual telltale signs of a feline intruder either: no smell of cat pee, no rodent remains, no makeshift bed. I even sent in Molly for a second time to double-check, and again she did the "down," even more confidently than before, perhaps, and earning herself a second batch of treats for yet another scent match.

"It's an absolute mystery," I said, scratching my head as Molly gratefully guzzled her black-pudding goodies.

I then tried a different angle. Sometimes, when I couldn't figure out why Molly was matching a scent or I couldn't find a cat in the vicinity, I'd verbally instruct her to "show me." This command, which I'd taught her at Bramble Hill Farm, required her to be more specific and, if need be, to physically guide me to the trigger.

In this instance, her response was to spin around and home in on the barn door. She nudged a small square of sky-blue material that was affixed to its handle before giving me another "down" for good measure (I was going to run out of treats, at this rate). I gently loosened the fabric swatch from the handle and held it up to a shaft of light streaming through the window.

"Why the heck is this bothering Molly?" I wondered, feeling totally mystified.

"Ah," said Godfrey, his face reddening slightly, "maybe I should have told you about that beforehand."

I swung around to face him. "Told me about what, Godfrey?"

"Well, um, I put that material there."

"You put it there? What on earth are you talking about?"

"Well, after I spoke to the farmer this morning, I came up with a brainwave. I thought it might be a good idea to cut up one of Edward's T-shirts and pin the pieces around this farmer's barns and stables. Sapphire might then recognize the scent and come out of hiding."

My aghast expression said it all.

"How many pieces did you put out, Godfrey?"

"Oh, I'd say about thirty. Did I do the wrong thing?"

"Er, you could say that."

It hadn't occurred to Godfrey that his "brainwave" had involved using an item of clothing from his car that had been contaminated with Sapphire's cat hair. Poor Molly had performed her duties perfectly—she'd correctly identified and isolated the cat's unique scent signature—but in this particular case it had led her straight to the T-shirt remnant.

This outcome, maddening though it was, only served to highlight Molly's fabulous knack of detecting one specific scent among a multitude of others. Canines have the remarkable ability to pinpoint and separate particular odors—much more so than any other species—something that was once explained to me with a perceptive analogy. If a human being entered a kitchen and a pot roast was on the stove, he or she would generally smell the overarching aroma of the dish. If a dog came into the kitchen, though, it would be able to scent-match each individual odor, distinguishing the beef from the bacon and the garlic from the onions. The most sensitive dogs' noses (like Molly's) would even have the capacity to scent-match the metal the pan was made out of. Staggering, really.

Godfrey had been very well intentioned, but wildly misguided; as a result, we'd wasted valuable time and I wasn't best pleased. I didn't make a big deal about it, though; my hyper-sensitive dog could easily detect bad vibes among humans, and it was vital that she remained upbeat and positive during a search. Instead, I politely asked Godfrey to collect and discard the rest of the T-shirt remnants so that we could restart our quest with a totally clean slate. By now I was pretty sure that the farmer's sighting was a false alarm anyway, since Molly had failed to detect any other notable scent trails. I needed to be certain that was the case, however. It took Molly a full hour to search the buildings, giving me total confidence that Sapphire was not in the area.

Edward joined us after lunch and had a few sharp words for his father when he learned of his faux pas.

He struck me as a pleasant, easygoing kind of guy—nowhere near as overbearing as Godfrey, mercifully—and we spent the rest of the afternoon combing the dock area for any signs of Sapphire (we still had several miles of riverbank to search). Despite her best efforts, Molly didn't detect a thing, unfortunately, and the rest of her treats remained in my pocket.

We rounded off a fairly frustrating day with a visit to the nearby general store and bakery, a mini-emporium of sweets, loaves and cakes owned by a friendly middle-aged couple. Experience had shown me that it was always a good idea to forge links with the village "hub"—it was normally the easiest way to spread the word and connect with the community—and this was no exception.

"Oh, I remember seeing her on the TV!" cooed the wife when I introduced her to Molly, while the husband gleefully brought out an ancient Kodak camera and began snapping away.

"Hey, it's not often that we have a celebrity in the shop," he grinned. "Say 'cheese,' Jean!"

They listened intently as we retold the story of Sapphire and the houseboat, and how Molly, the UK's first scent-matching cat-detection dog (I liked to shoe-horn that into the conversation), was endeavoring to find her in the village. The couple kindly promised to alert all their customers—we left a pile of leaflets near the cash register—and, as we waved goodbye, they told us we were always welcome to pop in for some home-made lemonade or some freshly baked flapjacks.

"See you soon, Molly, and good luck with finding Sapphire," they said, waving from behind the counter.

"Do people always go this loopy over your dog?" asked Edward, laughing.

"For the most part, yes." I smiled and explained how Molly garnered fans everywhere she went, wowing them with her talents and wooing them with her personality. During searches, she had this amazing ability to unite and rally a community: Neighbors would become totally invested in our "story" and would go above and beyond to help us find the cat and solve the mystery. "People love a happy ending, Edward," I said, "and I just hope we get one with Sapphire."

As we exited the shop, I noticed that the sunlight had begun to fade and the air had started to cool. Molly was looking tired—her head was starting to drop—and she needed some rest. She'd had a busy working day—albeit fruitless—and it was time to head back home.

I planned to return to Berkshire the following morning, however. Throughout the journey home, I kept having visions of a bedraggled little cat scrambling up a riverbank, exhausted from her tiring swim across the Thames. My gut feeling told me that Sapphire was still out there and I was determined to reunite her with her owners.

"As I've already said, Molls, cats can swim," I murmured as her gentle snores emanated from the back of the car.

Molly and I began day two with a house-to-house investigation along Hurley's winding country lanes, this time without Edward and Godfrey in tow. The latter was just too exhausting. On the previous day, he'd even started using some of my search commands with Molly, to which she'd responded by looking at him as if to say, *Hey, cut it out, I'm trying to work here.* I tactfully suggested that father and son were best deployed by the marina, where they could continue to engage with homeowners and holidaymakers.

"Ring me if you get any fresh leads or sightings, and I'll be straight over," I said.

"No problem," replied Edward. "We'll keep you posted."

Once I'd reintroduced Sapphire's scent to Molly, I began the usual knocking on doors, ringing on bells and pressing on buzzers. We searched half a dozen more gardens—no sign of any Sapphire scent, sadly— before reaching the corner property at the end of the lane. The door was answered by a lady sporting a floral dress and a floppy straw sunhat with silk flowers around the brim. She thought we were joking at first ("A pet detective? Really? Is this *Candid Camera*?") but eventually waved us into a large back garden that—like her outfit—was ablaze with summer flowers.

I let Molly off her leash and gave her freedom to roam. A grid of gravel pathways divided the immaculate lawn into four square sections; at its center, surrounded by low rose bushes, was a two-tiered, green-tinted fountain. It was a ghastly-looking thing—it had stone serpents and lizards wrapped around its base and a gargoyle's head as its spout—and it seemed totally incongruous among this fragrant oasis.

Molly must have built up a thirst, however, because she began to circle the fountain with intent. Before I could call her off—I wasn't sure how clean the water was—she took a short run up and, her paws gripping the second tier, took a giant slurp from the gargoyle spout. As she did so, I noticed the base starting to wobble ominously.

"Molly, OFF!" I shouted, sprinting toward her. But it was too late. I heard an enormous crack as the fountain keeled backward, smashing onto the stone beneath it and breaking into two. A petrified Molly swerved out of the way just in time and promptly bolted across the lawn. Having no doubt heard all the kerfuffle, the owner came dashing out, her dress billowing behind her.

Marvelous, I thought, my heart sinking. *That's another fine mess you've gotten me into, Molly . . .*

"Oh my goodness, you've broken my fountain!" she cried, looking first at the smashed-up ornament and then straight at me.

"It wasn't actually me, to be fair," I replied, with an apologetic shrug. "It was my dog. It was an accident. She was trying to get some water and, well, the whole thing just toppled over."

The woman stared at me, disbelief written all over her face, and then looked at Molly, who was now sitting upright, all prim and proper, a veritable picture of innocence. My dog had sold me out.

"Listen, I'm truly sorry about your fountain," I said. "Please tell me how much it'll cost to replace and I'll pay for it."

The lady took another look at the pretty cocker spaniel in her midst, paused for thought, then gave me a resigned smile.

"No, there'll be no need for that. It was, as you say, an accident. These things happen."

"Well, that's very decent of you. Thank you."

"To be honest," she continued, "I detest that fountain. It was a wedding present from my mother-in-law—spitting image of that gargoyle, if truth be told—and

I've been wanting to get rid of it ever since my divorce came through. You've probably done me a favor. My gardener's coming later, he'll gladly take it away for me."

"But only if you're sure . . ."

"Yes, I'm sure. Now, hang fire for a moment, and I'll bring that delightful dog of yours some proper water."

As she sashayed toward the house Molly sidled over to me and put a paw on my boot.

"Right, that's quite enough drama for one morning, young lady," I said as her big brown eyes stared up at me. It was at times like these I was reminded that, beneath that professional veneer, my dog could be as cheeky and mischievous as any other pooch.

We stopped at a village pub for something to eat and, taking advantage of the warm, sunny weather, I opted to sit on the veranda overlooking the Thames. As Molly devoured her doggy energy bar, I ate my plowman's lunch and watched the barges cruise along the river, returning friendly waves to any pleasure-boaters who offered them. I also noticed a few barges docking at the local RV park, located half a mile or so downstream.

"Eat up, Molls," I said, eyeing the rows of mobile homes as the sunlight glinted off their metal roofs. "I reckon that should be our next port of call."

Fortunately for us, as it was in the midst of the summer season, most of the cabins and RVs were occupied. Some were home to permanent residents but the majority were inhabited by vacationers enjoying some Thames-side downtime. A quick scan of the site revealed plenty of potential hiding places for a sanctuary-seeking cat—a door left ajar, a raised area of decking, a tarpaulin-covered trailer—although Molly's indifferent body language told me that there were no feline scent trails to excite her.

As we made our way through the park I engaged with as many people as possible, showing them Sapphire's photo and asking if they'd happened to have spotted a beautiful British Blue moseying by.

"Ah, what a lovely kitty, but, no, I haven't seen anything," said a suntanned woman lounging with a stack of glossy magazines by her feet. She and her husband had taken early retirement, she told me, and they spent the summer months in the luxury mobile home they'd bought with their savings.

"We're outside all the time, so I'm pretty sure I'd have seen a cat passing."

"If you could keep an eye out, that would be great," I said.

My next encounter was with a kayak-carrying family of four who were heading for some fun on the river. Once the boy and girl had given Molly a fuss—youngsters were drawn to her like a magnet—I inquired about Sapphire.

"No, sorry, not seen a cat around here, I'm afraid," said the father, shaking his head. I handed him a leaflet and my business card and asked him to get in touch with either myself or Edward, should they happen to spot her.

"And guess what," I said to the children as they tickled Molly's chin. "If either of you find Sapphire the cat, I'll make sure Molly brings you the biggest bag of sweets in the whole wide world as a reward. Deal?"

"Deal!" yelled the boy, giving me a high five.

"Deal!" giggled his little sister. "Can we go and look for Sapphire now, Daddy?"

As the family went on their merry way, my mobile phone rang. It was Edward.

"Colin, you need to come over to the marina, quickly," he said breathlessly. "We've found someone who thinks he might have seen Sapphire."

Within twenty minutes, Molly and I were sitting on a picnic bench with Edward, Godfrey, a gentleman named Jack and his big black Labrador, Solomon. A shaggy-haired, bushy-bearded hulk of a man, Jack had worked as Hurley's resident "riverbank man" for over twenty years. Most importantly, he knew every inch of the riverbank, right up to the border with Henley. His job entailed collecting fees from boat and barge owners, which he often did in the early hours, before people had the chance to skulk off without paying.

"Okay, Jack," I said, cutting to the chase. "Tell me what you know."

"Well, this morning—must have been about six o'clock—I was walking along the towpath a mile or so upriver, collecting a few fees, and Solomon suddenly started to strain on his leash."

His Labrador growled at the mention of his name, causing Molly to balk slightly.

"He then started to drag me away from the path, toward the long grass, and as we approached an old fallen oak tree I saw a cat," said Jack. "It just sat there and watched us, bold as brass. It even started licking its paws, but it didn't once take its eyes off Solomon."

On hearing his name again, the big Lab let out another grizzly growl. Molly looked at him as if to say, *Okay, buddy, that's quite enough of the growling . . .*

"How would you describe the cat, Jack?"

"Dark gray coat, bright green eyes, a bit skinny."

"And there are no other similar-looking cats in the neighborhood?"

"Nah. I know all the pets in the area. I've lived here years, walked the same route every day. Never seen it before in my life."

I showed him another photo of Sapphire. (I always

liked to have a few extra images of the missing cat for this very reason; it enabled me to assess the reliability of the sighting.)

"Did it look like this?"

He produced some reading glasses from the pocket of his lumberjack shirt and studied Sapphire's photo.

"Yes, I'm pretty sure that's the cat I saw."

Edward took a sharp intake of breath. "D'you think it's Sapphire?" he said. "D'you reckon she's still alive?"

"It's encouraging news, certainly," I replied, "but there's only one way we'll know for sure."

I took the all-important jam jar from my utility belt and crouched down next to Molly.

"We really need your help now, sweetheart," I whispered with affection. "Just do your best."

I asked Jack to take Solomon home (I feared his dog would distract Molly), but within minutes the riverbank man had returned to guide us along the towpath.

As we approached the fallen tree—it rested on a grassy knoll to the right of the path—I offered Molly the sample. Luckily, there'd been no rain for days, so I hoped that any lingering odor would remain strong enough for her to make a scent match.

The air was heavy with hope and expectation and the three men watched on, agog, as my smart little spaniel stuck her snout deep into the jar, her tail wagging like crazy.

Responding to my usual "Seek, seek" command, Molly raced into the long grass, springing high and squatting low as she traced the rise and fall of the riverside breeze. Then, suddenly, she homed in on the upended oak tree and—*bang!*—hit the deck immediately before giving me a textbook "down." She locked her brown, unblinking eyes on mine, as if to say, *FOUND IT, EVERYONE!*

"My god, that's exactly where I saw the cat," gasped Jack.

"Well, there you have it," I whispered to a wide-eyed, open-mouthed Edward. "Molly's signaling that Sapphire was definitely here this morning. She's telling us that your cat is still alive and well and that she clearly made it to the riverbank."

At this, Edward squealed with glee and threw his arms around his father, who somewhat stiffly returned the embrace.

"This is the best news ever!" he cried. "I need to call Lily."

Edward relayed the good news to his girlfriend, Jack headed off to the river to collect more fees and I gave Molly a run-around in a nearby clearing. Godfrey strode over to join us and watched Molly leaping into the air, trying to catch the insects that she'd disturbed. The old man seemed uncharacteristically muted, I noticed.

"Everything okay, Godfrey? You've gone all quiet."

"I'm at a loss for words, to be honest," he replied, with a slight catch in his voice. "I've seen lots of amazing things in my life, Mr. Butcher, but nothing quite like that. Your dog is truly incredible."

Witnessing Molly's unique talents for the first time could be quite an emotional experience for some people, even smart alecks like Godfrey.

"That's very kind of you to say," I said as my dog bounded back, her snout and paws sopping wet from the long meadow grass. "She's a very special dog."

We reconvened at the riverside picnic bench, beneath which an exhausted Molly fell into a deep sleep, emitting the occasional snort. Edward's and Godfrey's faces fell, however, when I explained that she'd reached her working time limit and that we'd soon have to head home to Sussex. While I appreciated their desire to find Sapphire—particularly now it seemed she was alive—the snakebite incident had made me super-cautious and Molly's welfare had to take priority.

I didn't leave without giving them some advice, though, or without explaining my theory as to how the cat had gone missing. Indeed, the situation had all become very Sherlock Holmes because, thanks to Molly's positive scent identification, we were now dealing with a "howdunnit." How had Sapphire reached dry land? How had she managed to stay safe in the meantime? How were we going to locate her?

"I reckon she did indeed fall overboard, perhaps not long after you set sail," I told Edward. "I think she then swam ashore, perhaps navigating her way to the dock you'd stayed at."

"And what then?"

"I suspect she just started to migrate in a random fashion, perhaps following some easy terrain, or a lit-up area."

"Like the towpath?"

"Yes, exactly. I imagine she'd have been drawn to the lights of the barges rather than the dark of the woods, put it that way. Displaced cats will always seek out human contact. They have a knack of finding other animal-lovers."

I unfurled my map of the area, using a marker pen to indicate the likely routes that Sapphire may have taken since the sighting, and slid it across the table to Edward.

"Don't give up," I said. "I'm confident you'll find her soon. Let me know how you get on this afternoon and we will see you again tomorrow morning."

"I will do," said Edward with a nod and a smile. "And thank you."

At around midnight, while I was reading in bed, with Sarah sleeping soundly beside me, I heard my phone buzzing in my bedside cabinet. It was Edward.

"I know it's late, and I'm sorry if I've woken you up," he said, "but I wanted you to hear this."

"Hear what?" I replied, puzzled.

"Sapphire. She's purring. She's sitting on my knee, and she's purring—"

"You found her?" I yelled as poor Sarah awoke with a start.

"What's happened?" she asked, rubbing her eyes.

"Sapphire's turned up," I whispered, only for my girlfriend to roll over, muttering something about a grown man getting excited about a missing cat.

"Yep. We found her," continued Edward. "Isn't it incredible?" It turned out that, earlier in the evening, he'd received a call from a vacationer at the RV site whose young daughter had heard a cat meowing as she'd settled down to sleep. The man had searched the mobile home from top to bottom—including all cupboards, wardrobes and drawers—but had been unable to locate it. It was only when he'd gone outside, armed with a flashlight, that he'd spied a pretty, dark gray cat hiding in a cavity beneath the RV. Certain it was the missing cat on the leaflet given to him by the pet detective and his dog, he'd called the owner's number straightaway.

"An hour later I had Sapphire in my arms," said Edward, his voice wavering with emotion. "Hungry and flea-ridden, but alive and kicking."

"That's fantastic news," I replied. "I'm so pleased for you all."

"I just had to ring you. I couldn't go without saying a huge thank-you to you and your fabulous dog. It was Molly who gave us that glimmer of hope, that impetus to carry on, and we'll never, ever forget that."

"Ah, thanks, Edward," I said, "and you're right, Molly is a remarkable dog. I can't wait to tell her the glad tidings in the morning."

"Oh, and one last thing," added my client. "The little girl in the RV asked me when she'd be getting the biggest bag of sweets in the whole wide world."

"Ha, I forgot about that." I laughed. "I'll sort out some kind of treat, don't worry."

After ending the call, I switched off the bedside light, laid my head back on the pillow and smiled contentedly. While I was slightly disappointed that Molly hadn't made the actual find, hearing the relief and happiness in Edward's voice was ample compensation. My thoughts switched to my spaniel, curled up in her bed downstairs, and I wondered how aware my little heroine was of her extraordinary ability to bring people, and their pets, together.

I'm so incredibly lucky to have her, I thought before drifting off to sleep.

13

A MISSING CAT AND A GRUMPY NEIGHBOR

Life as a cat-detection dog could get quite exhausting, and it was vitally important that Molly received plenty of downtime. After most searches I gave her a rest day, allowing her a long, undisturbed sleep, a lazy hang around the house (often with her soft toy rabbit in tow) and, just before dinner, a leisurely walk in the woods. If it was a summer's day, Molly would invariably find the warmest place in the house for a spot of sunbathing; like many cats and dogs, she loved basking smack-dab in the middle of the brightest shaft of sunlight.

Molly would usually spend her days off with me but, if I ever had any private-investigation duties to attend to, Sarah would step in. This was indeed the case in late September 2017, when a client of mine asked Stefan and me to conduct a surveillance operation. I finally returned home at nine o'clock that evening—the job had been a long, drawn-out affair—but any stresses and strains evaporated as soon as I opened the front door.

There before me, in the living room, lay a vision of domestic bliss. Sarah was curled up on the sofa with a book, and wrapped around her feet was a snoozing, snoring Molly. I couldn't help but smile. Once upon a time, Sarah—an avowed cat-lover—could hardly bear to be within a yard of this hair-shedding, handbag-snuffling rescue mutt, but now here they were, snuggling together like a pair of old friends.

"Well, well, well . . . just look at you two," I grinned, feeling all aglow. "Who'd have thought it, eh?"

"We've had the best girly day out ever," beamed Sarah, gazing fondly at Molly as she slept beside her.

Sarah and Molly—friends at last

"Shopping in Guildford, lunch in Cranleigh and a work-out on the common. We've not missed you one jot, Colin."

"Well, that's just charming," I said, rolling my eyes in mock indignation.

In reality, I was beyond thrilled to see my two favorite girls getting along so well and appearing so calm and comfortable in each other's company. I had been Sarah's biggest fan since the day we'd first met, but to see her bonding so beautifully with Molly only strengthened my feelings of respect and gratitude. Giving my dog a loving and caring home was so important to me, on both a personal and a professional level and—that evening—it felt like the final piece of the jigsaw was in place.

I hung up my coat, lit a fire, made us coffee and sat down on the rug in front of Molly. She soon sensed my presence, awoke from her slumbers and, after giving me a sleepy lick, jumped up and climbed into my lap.

"Okay, missy, you can have a ten-minute cuddle, but then it's definitely time for bed," I said, kissing her snout. "We've got an early start tomorrow morning—we're traveling south—and I need you to be bright-eyed and bushy-tailed."

A ginger tomcat, Simba, had gone missing in Devon (I'd received the SOS call earlier that day) and the owners were desperate for our help. As with so many of our cases, marvelous Molly was their only remaining hope.

We arrived a little earlier than planned—the roads had been nice and quiet—so we stopped off for a quick coffee and scone at a local café and, within minutes, Molly had all the staff doting on her.

Then, as always, we undertook a pre-search walkabout, observing the layout of the roads and the location of buildings, as well as any hazards or obstacles that might put Molly at risk. As we ambled around the country lanes, it was clear that we were in picture-postcard territory. Thatched cottages lined the maze of cobbled streets and at the heart of the village lay a church, a monument, and a duck pond, complete with floating lily pads.

As we began to make our way back to the car, we heard a *clippety-clop* of hooves. Emerging around the corner, riding a dark brown horse, was a woman wearing riding clothes and boots. This striking-looking lady was flanked by two stocky Irish wolfhounds, running fast and loose, their pink tongues lolling. Molly sat down and watched the trio and their owner shoot past.

Wow, what was that, Dad? she seemed to be saying.

"Good morning to you," said the woman, smiling and slowing down slightly. "Have a super day!"

With a dig of the heels and a tug of the reins, she galloped along the lane, her doggy duo cavorting behind her.

Chugging in the opposite direction, past the old schoolhouse, came an old tractor towing a trailer packed with apple crates. The flat-capped farmer at the wheel honked his horn and raised his palm in acknowledgment, as if he'd known us all his life.

"Remind me again, Colin, which year have we traveled back to?" joked Sam.

"Nineteen fifty-eight, I reckon." I winked.

Half an hour later I was knocking on the door of a stone cottage, where Lindsey, Simba's owner, was staying. Molly and Sam remained in the car, as they often did while I interviewed the family and obtained the cat-hair sample.

A slight girl in her early teens, Lindsey had been lodging with her family friend while her mother and father were on vacation. I gathered she'd been recovering from a serious illness—I didn't pry any further—and that her parents had preferred not to leave her alone.

To say that Lindsey adored her chubby, cheeky ginger tom was an understatement. They were simply inseparable. Rescued ten years previously from a cat shelter,

Simba had been a constant presence during Lindsey's childhood and had been a source of comfort and affection as she'd battled through some tough times. Other than a long-held love of reading, spending quality time with her noisy and mischievous furball was one of her favorite hobbies, and she'd spend hours testing his dexterity with Ping-Pong balls or teasing him with a medley of fluffy cat toys.

During the warmer months Lindsey would sit with Simba in the garden, reading one of her favorite historical novels as he lazed in the sunshine. Occasionally, the cat would spring into action if a robin or song thrush dared to hop onto his patch—despite his advancing years (and impressive weight), his hunting instinct remained strong—but Lindsey's shrill cry of "Simba!" would usually distract the animals and avert a skirmish. She was also mindful of the fact that her father was a keen birdwatcher who never appreciated lifeless, feathery "gifts" being delivered through the cat flap.

With his owner by his side, Simba initially seemed to have settled into his new environment. Lindsey had kept him indoors at first, but after the first week had caved in to his constant back-door scratching and had let him out to explore. Within a few days, however, her cherished pet had gone missing and her world had fallen apart.

Upon hearing the news her mother and father, Wendy and Chris, had flown home from their vacation to join the search for Simba. Having combed the village's cobbled streets and back gardens, they'd hit a metaphorical brick wall and, having read about Molly in a newspaper, her dad had decided to give UK Pet Detectives a call.

"My daughter is fragile enough at the best of times," he'd explained, "but Simba going AWOL has got her teetering on the brink. She's devoted to him, Mr. Butcher, and we desperately need your help to find him."

The area was way beyond my usual boundaries, but due to the delicate nature of the case I agreed to lend a hand. I hoped the compact nature of the village would work in our favor, since there'd only be a relatively small number of buildings to search. Also, since Simba had gone missing from a single-pet household, I was confident that we'd be able to extract a high-quality hair sample, which would benefit Molly's scent-matching process.

Unsurprisingly, the atmosphere around the breakfast table that morning was tense. A teary Lindsey was inconsolable.

I felt it was important to add some context to Simba's disappearance, so I explained that there were generally two causes for a pet to go missing. Either outside forces beyond the control of the owner, such as an aggressive dog moving in next door, fireworks being set off in a local park, or construction workers digging up a nearby road. Or more personal reasons—which applied to Simba, I believed—such as the arrival of a new pet or baby, an unwanted change in diet or, as in this case, a disorienting house move.

I guessed that Simba had been unsettled by the move to the family friend's house and had escaped at the first opportunity.

And then I added that sometimes a cat will return home on its own.

"Oh, please let that be the case," said Lindsey, managing a weak smile as she blotted her damp cheeks with a handkerchief. With my client feeling a little more optimistic, I went upstairs to the spare room to collect the required cat hair from Simba's fleecy blanket.

Chris asked if he could join us on the search for Simba—he was anxious to help, and I knew his local knowledge would prove invaluable—while Wendy remained at the house with her daughter. As soon as he unlatched the front door, however, it was abundantly clear that we had a huge problem. Plumes of smoke billowed from a nearby field and the air was heavy with the acrid smell of burning wood. It seemed a local farmer had lit an early-morning bonfire.

"I don't want to alarm you, Chris, but Molly won't be able to work today if that fire continues to rage," I said. "It'll badly affect her sense of smell and it'll mask the cat scent."

"Leave this to me," hissed Chris. "I know that farmer. I'm going to give him a piece of my mind. He shouldn't be lighting fires at this time of day, anyway."

The farmer reluctantly agreed to quell the fire, but we had to wait an hour for the smoke to disperse before we could commence the search. We made good use of the time by walking around the village and introducing ourselves to more passersby. Once the bonfire fumes had finally dissipated, I gave Molly the green light to inhale Simba's scent and we began the search in earnest.

We soon approached a beautiful stone property, its grounds full of trees, and were greeted in the driveway by the owner. The way he kept his distance from Molly suggested that he wasn't a dog-lover.

"Search away, by all means," he said, after we'd introduced ourselves and explained our circumstances, "but please don't let your dog anywhere near my pond. I keep koi carp, you see; they're very sensitive fish and I don't want them being startled."

He was about to head back to his house when he stopped in his tracks, as if he'd just remembered something.

"Oh, I forgot . . . you need to keep an eye out for our three-foot hedgehog, too."

"Excuse me?" I replied. Either this guy had gotten his woodland animals mixed up or he was off his rocker.

"Yeah, there's a three-foot hedgehog that often visits at this time of year." He nodded earnestly. "Mrs. Bumble, I call her. Hunts around the logs and tree stumps for slugs and snails, and I leave out bowls of water for her. I wouldn't like her to get spooked by your dog, so please do be careful."

"We will, don't worry," I said as Sam rolled her eyes and stifled a giggle.

"Beware of gentle fish and giant hedgehogs . . . is he for real?" she whispered.

I let Molly off her leash and, with Simba's scent still pervading her nostrils, she charged around the garden, snuffling beneath shrubs, sniffing around tree trunks and scattering leaves in her wake like confetti. At one point she raced over to the koi-carp pond, impishly dipping in her paw before my cry of "Molly, OFF!" diverted her from the fluorescent fish gliding beneath. They seemed completely unfazed by the intrusion, however, and several of them surfaced to see if there was any food on offer.

Then, about ten minutes into the search, my dog's body language and behavior pattern completely changed. She became quite hyperactive, bouncing on her front paws, scampering back and forth in a state of mild confusion and making weird snorting noises. She had detected some kind of scent trail, but her lack of certainty—and the absence of a meaningful "down"—suggested that it didn't belong to Simba the cat.

She then began to circle a large mound of soggy oak leaves. Chris, Sam and I edged closer, nudging each other as we saw something moving sideways beneath it. Suddenly, a large, up-turned plastic bowl emerged and began to shimmy toward the back wall, as if it were being remotely controlled. Molly went totally haywire, whinnying loudly, spinning around in circles and rearing up on her hind legs like a fretful foal. For her own safety—and conscious of the house-owner's twitching curtains—I recalled my dog immediately and reattached her leash, handing her over to Sam while I investigated further. I crept over to the bowl, carefully lifted it up and, lo and behold, there sat a quaking little hedgehog. It contracted into a tight ball—the normal defense mechanism—but by then I'd already noticed its back foot was missing. It only had three legs. Mrs. Bumble, it appeared, was a three-footed hedgehog, not a three-foot hedgehog. I chuckled to myself—*had I really expected to discover a hedgehog bigger than Molly?*—and gave the spiny creature the gentlest of prods, so that it lopsidedly scuttled under a nearby holly bush, out of my dog's eye-line. I refilled Mrs. B's feeding bowl with the water bottle in my utility belt and ambled back up the garden.

"Well, you've unearthed one cute little animal," I said to Molly. "Let's just hope the next one's Simba."

While we'd managed to comb much of the village, by lunchtime Molly hadn't gotten a sniff of Simba, quite literally. When we resumed the search, however—down the quaintly named Honeysuckle Lane—she became very interested in the old drainage system that ran beneath some of the back gardens and was exposed in others (among them the garden from which Simba had escaped). While it wasn't safe enough for me to allow Molly to run through this cracked, crumbling pipeline, her tail wagged like crazy whenever she got near it. I couldn't help but wonder whether any local cats— more specifically Simba—had used it as a convenient little tunnel between gardens.

Much to my chagrin, the drain pipe opened out into a yard that we'd been unable to access. My numerous raps on the front door had remained unanswered, yet I'd noticed a shadowy presence hovering behind the cream-colored net curtains and seen the flicker of a television screen. Someone was definitely inside but, for whatever reason, they hadn't wanted to come out. In normal circumstances, I'd have just shrugged my shoulders and moved on to the next house, but Molly was champing at the bit to explore this particular property.

"Oh, you mean Old Mr. Grumpy?" two teenage boys had sniggered when I'd asked about the cottage's owner. "He only ever comes out to tell us to stop playing football or to clear off home."

I wasn't going to be deterred, regardless of Old Mr. Grumpy's reputation, and in spite of the two locked and bolted wrought-iron gates that blocked entry to his garden.

With Molly leading the way, and with Chris and Sam by my side, I followed the narrow passageway that separated the back gardens from the village cemetery and peeked over this gentleman's fence. Parked in his driveway was an orange Volkswagen van—vintage, but pristine—and in his garden lay three immaculate sheds. Wooden bird feeders were dotted around the rectangular lawn, a third of which was devoted to a neat fruit and vegetable patch.

As we admired Mr. Grumpy's garden, Molly was becoming increasingly uptight—she was continuously pawing at the back fence—and I realized it was time for action.

"Right, we need to find a way to gain access," I said. "This guy's not answering his front door, so we're going to have to bend the rules a little."

Sam and I gave Chris a leg up over the fence and into the garden—not difficult, since he was a very slim and wiry guy—and I asked him to go and rap on Mr. Grumpy's back door. (I reckoned he'd respond more favorably to a local.)

After five minutes of constant knocking, Chris finally got a response.

"All right, all right, I can bloody hear you," a gruff voice shouted from behind the door as we heard a key turning in the lock and a succession of bolts being undone. Standing there, with a face like thunder, was a burly fellow in his early eighties, with thinning salt-and-pepper hair.

"What d'you think you're playing at, climbing over my fence?" he snapped.

"Well, er . . . ," stammered Chris, slightly taken aback by this imposing figure of a man.

"Are you police or something?" continued Old Mr. Grumpy, gesturing at me and Sam as we lurked behind his gate.

"Well, not exactly," replied Chris falteringly, "but I'm wondering if you could kindly unlock the gate so my colleagues can have a quick word."

"It had better be quick," he scowled, producing a huge set of keys from his pocket and pacing toward the gate. "I'm a busy man. Got stuff to do."

So far, so good—Chris had managed a tricky situation well—but it was now time for me to launch a full-on charm offensive.

After endlessly complimenting his garden, I got him to relax. So I proceeded to tell him all about Molly—who was being valiantly reined in by Sam—and described our painstaking search for poor Simba.

"We're looking for a ginger tomcat," I said. "He's a bit old, and a bit plump, but he's still quite a lively chap. We think he might have been using the old drainage pipe to travel between gardens and might well have ended up in yours."

"My daughter's missing him so much," added Chris, showing him a photograph, "so if you'd let us have a look around, we'd be most grateful."

"Well, I never!" he exclaimed, squinting at the picture. "I've definitely seen that cat."

"Really?" Chris gasped.

"Oh, yes, I thought it was a stray. He's been here every morning for the last few days. Bit of a pest, to be honest. Keeps bothering the sparrows and blue birds. Tried to jump on my bird feeder yesterday, but he was so fat it toppled over."

"That sounds just like our Simba," said Chris excitedly. "Can we start looking now?"

"Feel free." The man hesitated for a couple of seconds and then added, "Not that you'll find him here now, though. He usually pops over before breakfast. I never see him in the afternoon."

I released Molly from her leash and, like a greyhound chasing a hare, she shot off toward the middle shed. She skidded to a halt in front of the dark green door, whirled around a few times and—*bang!*—performed the mother of all "downs."

"What on earth is she doing?" asked the man as Molly adopted her sphinx pose, shuddering with excitement.

"Molly's telling me that she has scent-matched Simba's smell," I explained, reaching into my utility belt for Molly's black-pudding treats. "And that means the cat is either inside that shed right now or was in there earlier."

"But that's where I keep my lawnmowers," he said, delving for his keys once again. "I can't imagine a cat would want to go in there. And I certainly didn't notice anything when I went in this morning."

He opened the shed door and I kept a close eye on Molly as she crossed the threshold. Inside was a shiny orange riding mower, a couple of old wooden benches and various bags and containers. I was confident that my dog's nose would be able to discern Simba's scent through the damp, tangy smell of cut grass mixed with the aroma of engine oil, and she didn't disappoint. In the far corner of the shed, beneath a gaping window, Molly gave us yet another positive, definitive signal. There was no trace of the cat himself, unfortunately—although judging from Molly's animated body language I reckoned that we'd only just missed him.

I dropped another handful of treats in front of Molly and as I did so, I noticed a half-eaten can of tuna under one of the benches. I looked at the man, who by now had told us his name was Alf, and he turned away furtively. Not wanting to embarrass him in front of Chris, I said, "Okay, Sam, if you and Chris search the front of the property, Molly and I will search behind these sheds."

After completing the search of the rear garden, Alf kindly let me give Molly a run-around on his patio— play was always part of the reward process—but only if I kept her away from his veg patch.

Once I had tired her out and given her some water, I joined Alf on his patio bench and we chatted about his life in the village.

When a tired-out Molly pushed herself between the two of us, Alf gave her an affectionate pat.

And then he loosened up a little and began telling me that following his wife's death he'd become very lonely.

While we were sitting there, my walkie-talkie spluttered into action.

"Colin, are you there?" yelled a frantic-sounding Sam.

"Yes, I'm right here," I said, lifting up the handset. "Whatever's the matter?"

"Oh my god, you're never going to believe this, but I can see Simba."

"What?"

"Seriously. He's at the gate in front of Alf's house as I speak. What should we do?"

"Sam, it's really important that you both remain calm and maintain your distance. We don't want the cat getting spooked and hurtling off. Stay right there and leave this to me."

I put Molly on a short leash and gave her the hand-down signal, which meant stay calm. I then crept around the side of the house, as stealthily as I could, and there—coolly padding along the front garden wall, with his head held high and his tail pointing north—was the unmistakable sight of Simba. He saw me advancing toward the wall, made a funny little *brrrrrrp* sound and swaggered over. This was no knock-kneed scaredy-cat.

With Chris and Sam looking on nervously, I gently inched toward Simba and lifted up my hand to stroke him. He brushed his head under my palm a couple of times, giving me a snuffle and a lick for good measure. He then looked down at Molly, who was standing there quietly, and meowed. I nodded to Sam, who slowly stepped forward and lifted Simba off the wall. Nobody said a word but, as the cat rested his front paws on my colleague's shoulders and nuzzled into her neck, the air crackled with emotion. The cat had been found, and Lindsey's nightmare was over.

Sam handed Simba to Chris, then took Molly back to the car and, after bidding Alf a fond farewell, Chris and I took the short walk to the family friend's cottage. Simba was happily ensconced in Chris's arms.

As news of his recovery swept through the village, a string of locals emerged from doorways.

But the biggest fanfare of all took place back at the house, where a beaming Lindsey finally clapped eyes on her precious Simba.

"I thought you'd gone forever!" she squealed, flinging her arms around him and smothering him in kisses. "You'll never know how much I missed you."

With the objective met, it was time for me to say my goodbyes and head back to Molly. Before I did so, however, I asked a favor of the family.

"This is just a suggestion, and please don't feel obliged, but I think it might be nice if you popped in to see Alf at some point," I said.

"Old Mr. Grumpy?" said Chris. "Are you serious?"

"His bark's much worse than his bite, I can assure

you," I said, smiling, "and we have a lot to thank him for. Had he not allowed Molly in his garden, we might have been forced to look elsewhere, and we might never have found Simba."

"We'll pay him a visit, for sure," said Lindsey. "It's the least we can do."

After we got home Molly badly needed to stretch her legs.

As I leaned against an oak tree and gazed across at my lovely little dog, I thought about that day's adventure and reflected upon Molly's amazing ability to charm everyone whose path she crossed. She attracted so much love and attention (why, even the koi carp had popped up to say hello). I allowed my crazy little dog a few more minutes to chase field mice she'd never catch before calling her back to my side.

"Time for your beauty sleep, missus," I said. "Let's head back home."

THE RUNAWAY BRIXTON TOMCAT

Many of our missing-pet searches took place in London, and whenever Molly and I visited the capital she always created a bit of a stir. Everywhere we went people would always stop to fuss at her. At first I used to think they were gravitating to her because she was so sweet-looking, but then I realized that my super-clever, attention-craving dog was almost mesmerizing them. She would often use eye contact with passersby to encourage interaction, and few could resist stopping and petting her once she locked her big brown eyes with theirs. Tourists from overseas, especially, seemed to adore her.

We have traveled all over the city to hunt for lost pets, from an overly curious tabby we found locked in an empty house in Greenwich to a timid cat recovered from the engine of an abandoned van in Camden.

One particular search, based in northwest London,

resulted in a truly unexpected outcome. A couple had contacted me about their dog, a Patterdale terrier called Cola, who, one afternoon, had gone missing from their home. It turned out that a moving company had been in and out of the house all day (the owners, Trevor and Pamela, were temporarily moving out while some major renovation work was done) and their dog had scampered out of the front door.

"We reckon he's gone off chasing foxes," said Trevor. "It's hard-wired into his DNA, apparently."

It all sounded quite plausible; I'd come across Patterdale terriers before and was aware of their traits and tendencies. More of a "type" than a breed, they were originally reared by hunt masters to flush out foxes. However, after fox hunting was outlawed in 2004, the Patterdale became obsolete as a working dog and, due to its rather challenging behavior, was not the most popular choice of pet. Those owners that did take them on—like Trevor and Pamela—would soon discover that chasing foxes still remained second nature. On this particular occasion, Cola had gone missing for over a day and it was feared that a fox earth had collapsed on him, or he'd become trapped in it. I had dealt with a fair few cases of terriers getting stuck in fox dens, so for me it was not an uncommon case.

"If you gave your dog Cola's scent, do you think she'd be able to sniff him out?" asked Trevor during our initial phone conversation. I explained that Molly had been trained primarily as a cat-detection dog but that she had, in fact, been involved in successful searches for other missing dogs, notably Buffy.

"While I can't offer you any guarantees, we can certainly give it a go," I said, agreeing to drive over to his house the next day.

Trevor and his wife lived in a lavish private community of opulent mansions, some of which, he told me, were home to a variety of A-list celebrities. At one point we stopped to admire a particularly grand property—a huge, red-brick house—only to find ourselves being challenged by a security guard who'd spotted us on CCTV and asked to see our ID. It seemed that we'd chosen to loiter outside the Malaysian ambassador's residence. He eventually allowed us to go on our way, but not before he'd given Molly a lot of attention.

Molly proudly indicating that she's found a missing cat

"I used to work with cocker spaniel sniffer dogs many moons ago." He smiled as Molly placed a front paw on his foot. "Fantastic animals. Love them to bits. Fancy a job swap?"

"Not likely," I said, laughing.

Trevor explained that he'd spent the morning pinpointing many of the area's fox dens. There were dozens, I discovered, ranging from dens built underneath woodpiles to bolt-holes hollowed out from the soil. Trevor reckoned there could be up to forty hideaways in the area.

"You've got your work cut out here, missus," I said to Molly as she excitedly inhaled Cola's scent sample from the jam jar. I then allowed her to "run with her nose" (essentially giving her a free rein, with minimal direction) and we moved from one den to the next, as stealthily as possible so as not to disturb any occupants. Molly had been trained to be inconspicuous—she was incredibly discreet during searches—so she was able to do this brilliantly.

Three hours later, with the skies getting darker and the air becoming damper, we'd still not found any sign of Cola. As time marched on, and as Molly continued to hunt in vain, I began to suspect that Trevor's dog had ventured farther afield.

"Let's give it another twenty minutes, and then I'm afraid we'll have to call it a day."

"I totally understand, Colin," replied Trevor, somewhat despondently.

We approached a small glade that was carpeted with leaves, branches and fungi and shaded by an old horse-chestnut tree. Molly charged on ahead of us, kicking up twigs and flicking up toadstools, but as soon as she reached the tree she stopped in her tracks, wheeled herself around and locked her eyes with mine. Over the past year I'd learned to read Molly's body language and behavior, just as she had mine, and quite often there was no need for words because I could instinctively understand what she was telling me. From what I could gather here, she was indicating that she'd hit a strange, confusing odor, something that she wasn't altogether sure about.

I've detected something, but it's not the target scent . . . what d'you want me to do, Dad?

"What have you found, girl? Show me," I said, walking over to investigate.

All I could see was leaf matter—there were no objects or creatures of interest—so I decided to call Molly off. However, just as I was about to give her the command, she began to dig furiously, raking up the soil around her and thrusting her nose into the ever-deepening hole. All of a sudden, I saw her tugging something out with her teeth; it appeared to be a blue velvet bag, about the size of a hot-water bottle and encrusted in a thick layer of grime. Having managed to drag it out, Molly released her jaw and flung the bag across the ground and, as she did so, a variety of shiny, jangly items cascaded out and landed by my feet.

"Oh my goodness." Trevor laughed and surveyed the glinting pile of necklaces, rings and bracelets. "Your dog's sniffed out the Crown Jewels."

I gave Molly a small kibble treat (she was staring up at me beseechingly, clearly expecting a reward for her efforts) then told her to lie down while I explored further. I knelt on the ground, peered into the hole and scraped away at the soil with my fingers. Two minutes later I'd unearthed the remnants of two wooden jewelry boxes, both covered in soggy blue silk, which almost disintegrated when I gently lifted them to the surface. Molly's snout appeared under my arm—as always, curiosity had gotten the better of her—and she watched earnestly as I opened the boxes and, one by one, lifted out a selection of gold chains and pearl necklaces, as well as a handful of earrings, brooches and cuff links. Particularly eye-catching was a beautiful antique ring studded with tiny diamonds and rubies.

"Wow, just look at that, Molls!" I said as the ring's gemstones glimmered in the watery sunlight. "Someone out there is missing some lovely jewelry."

I carefully transferred our little haul into a carrier bag (I always kept one in my utility-belt pocket) and knotted it securely. It was at that juncture, when I felt

The treasures that Molly found on Hampstead Heath

Molly could do no more, that we had to bid a reluctant farewell to Trevor.

"I'm so sorry you didn't have the outcome you wanted," I said, shaking his hand, "but please keep me informed. I'm confident that Cola will come back at some point. And if you find any more fox earths in the area, don't hesitate to call me. I'd be more than happy to return with Molly."

"Ah, that's very kind," he replied, "and I sincerely appreciate everything you've both done today."

My perceptive little dog then stepped in close, leaned against his leg and let out a soft whine, as if she somehow understood the pain he was suffering.

While I was dreadfully disappointed that we hadn't located the dog, I was satisfied—as was Trevor, I think—that we'd done all we could in the circumstances. Molly had searched every single fox earth, which meant that our client had at least been able to go home knowing that the immediate area had been combed extensively and could still cling on to the hope that his dog was still alive, albeit farther afield.

⁓ ⁓ ⁓

The following morning, in the Bramble Hill Farm kitchen, Sam gave the jewelry a thorough clean and polish before laying it across the draining board to dry. Upon closer inspection, half of Molly's haul appeared to consist of decent-quality vintage pieces in gold and silver (some adorned with diamonds, rubies and semi-precious stones), with the rest comprising fairly chunky and garish costume jewelry.

Over the next few days I contacted a host of different people and places in an attempt to locate the jewelry's rightful owner. First and foremost, I reached out to the Malaysian ambassador's office, mindful of what the security guard had told me about the burglary. Had the thief buried the treasure in the woods, with a view to one day reclaiming it? Disappointingly, however, the staff chose not to return my numerous calls and emails, so I could only assume that I was wide of the mark.

I then contacted the Metropolitan Police, only to be told by a civilian operative that there was little point bringing it into the police station. There was no way of knowing how long the jewelry had lain hidden underground—and I didn't know for certain that it was stolen—so it would simply take too long to check through all the old crime reports.

"The best thing to do is hang on to them for the time being and try to find the owner," she said breezily. "If no one comes forward, then you can keep it."

My search continued regardless, and I circulated photos of some of the jewelry to the local newspapers and to community websites. I received a handful of inquiries in response, but they were largely opportunistic and nobody was able to verify ownership.

Back in the office, Sam and I made arrangements to send the gems to a local secondhand jewelry shop; the owner agreed to hang on to them until an owner came forward.

"So, as it stands, Molly, all this bling belongs to you," I grinned, balancing a dainty tiara between her floppy ears. "Finders, keepers, eh?"

As Sam took a photograph of a regal-looking Molly striking a pose, my phone rang. It was Trevor, passing on the marvelous news that Cola had returned home. His escapade had left him utterly exhausted, but he was safe and well.

"That's made my day, Trevor," I said, hearing the terrier yapping excitedly in the background.

In December 2017 I found myself in South London. The case this time was a missing cat, a marmalade-colored British shorthair named Columbus that belonged to a teenager, Harriet, who lived with her parents and four other cats. The story went that, one morning, the father—Kenneth—had been due to take Columbus to the vet for a routine checkup. Since it was a lovely crisp, cold and sunny winter's day, Kenneth had decided to go on foot instead of using the car. He had ushered a rather belligerent Columbus into a well-worn canvas pet carrier and had taken a shortcut through the local park. He had then walked out of the exit gate and switched the cat carrier to his right hand.

Just as Kenneth had approached the sliding door at the vet, a young man had rushed out, clinging desperately to a leash attached to a big, barking English setter. Anxious and agitated, the dog had taken one look at the cat carrier and, with a snarl, had forcefully shoved its snout into the mesh front. Poor Columbus must have been petrified.

Kenneth hurried toward the entrance, but Columbus's right paw suddenly clawed out of the netting. In the blink of an eye, the cat had ripped away a huge hole, muscled its way through and run off. Kenneth had tried to chase him, only to see Columbus disappear over a ten-foot wall. Despite the efforts of some helpful passersby, the cat couldn't be found anywhere.

Breaking the bad news to Harriet that afternoon had been traumatic. The young girl was beyond distressed, fearing that she'd never see her darling Columbus again.

～～～～～

For the next forty-eight hours they combed the busy streets, calling out Columbus's name until they were hoarse and handing out hastily printed CAT: MISSING leaflets. There were no confirmed sightings, sadly. Harriet explained to me that she had posted a Columbus-related appeal on social media, and one of the replies had suggested contacting "that pet-detective bloke with the dog who was on *This Morning*."

Harriet was in luck. Molly and I had just completed a two-hour training search—and I felt that this case was something we could definitely get our teeth into. There were, however, two areas of concern. First, our search area was built up and populous. Urban searches tended to be trickier and more time-consuming than their rural counterparts. My second reservation was that Columbus resided in a multi-cat household—he had four feline "siblings"—and if I couldn't locate a unique sample of his scent, then the search would simply not go ahead.

"I won't be long, sweetheart," I said to Molly as I pulled up outside Kenneth and Harriet's red-brick house. Our journey had taken us an hour and a half, and Molly was champing at the bit to get started, but—as always—it was important that I spent some time with the owners. I needed to glean as much information about their cat as possible, as well as obtaining a nice wad of Columbus's fur.

Harriet—a tall girl with auburn hair—told me that she'd had him since he was a kitten and, because he was always off exploring somewhere, had named him Columbus. Her cat was, by all accounts, a very confident and capable creature.

"Oh, no one messes with Columbus," said Harriet. "My other cats often bear the brunt of his temper."

She also told me that he hated attending his regular checkups at the vet, which made it fairly easy to identify the cause and trigger of his dash for freedom. The bumpy journey in a flimsy cat carrier would have sent Columbus's stress levels rocketing. Then, when he was confronted with the sight and scent of the dreaded vet, he'd been ready to make a break for it. The unwanted hairy dog snout had been the final straw and had triggered his frantic escape.

Twenty minutes later our search party—father, daughter, Molly and me—commenced the hunt for Columbus, all of us wearing thick, warm jackets to combat the wintry chill.

We headed to the vet to survey Columbus's escape route ("Wow, that's one agile cat," I said, when I spied the imposing wall) and decided to visit the properties that backed onto it. The vast majority of the shop-keepers and householders I encountered that day were extremely helpful and obliging.

This included the staff of a senior citizens' care home located in a handsome red-brick building which we visited about two hours into our search. With the sample scent still coursing through her nostrils, Molly had become rather animated as we'd walked up the driveway, so I was very keen to access its grounds. I stopped a senior nurse who was clocking on to her shift and, as luck would have it, she just happened to be a committed cat-lover. Her face fell when Harriet and I told her about Columbus's disappearance.

"Oh, that's so, so sad," she said. "Meet me around the back of the building and I'll let you through the gate. I'm not really supposed to do this, but in the circumstances . . ."

Molly and I began to search the care-home garden.

"The residents like to sit out here, especially when the sun's out," said the nurse, gesturing toward the wrought-iron chairs that were dotted around the perim-eter. "They like watching the garden grow . . ."

". . . and we love to see what's going in our vege-table soup, too," piped up a voice behind us. I swung around to see a tiny, gray-haired woman wearing a woolly purple coat and a matching beret. A pair of black-rimmed, thick-lensed spectacles dominated her face, giving her an almost cartoonish appearance.

"I'm Gracie," she said, smiling, and offered me a trembling handshake. "I saw your delightful little dog and I just had to come out and say hello."

Pets weren't allowed in the care home, but she told me how she tried to stay close to nature by filling up the birdbaths with fresh water, and by creeping into the garden every evening to feed cat food or dog food to the local hedgehogs, foxes and, occasionally, stray cats.

Cat food? I thought to myself. *The sooner we get this garden searched, the better . . .*

While Molly was as patient as ever, bless her, after a few minutes of fussing and petting from the old lady I could sense that, like me, she was itching to continue with our mission.

"It's been lovely talking to you, Gracie," I said, "but I'm afraid we need to crack on."

"Of course," she said. "I do hope you find Columbus the cat."

I reintroduced the sample scent to Molly, just for a quick turbo boost. She promptly skyrocketed to the far end of the garden and, after feverishly snuffling around a hole in a fence panel, gave me the most beautiful "down." As I edged closer, I could even spot stray wisps of ginger hair on the gap's jagged edges.

"Brilliant work, Molly," I said as she snarfed down some black-pudding titbits from the palm of my hand.

Kenneth and Harriet were thrilled at this positive development, and we popped back to their house for a debrief. I believed that Columbus had made his way into the care-home garden late at night before heading back to a place of shelter, perhaps deep within a nearby railway arch.

A nighttime stakeout at the care home wouldn't be possible, sadly; Molly had almost exceeded her maximum six-hours-a-day limit—any longer was too physically demanding—and I'd soon have to take her back to Cranleigh. As an alternative, I decided to rig up a network of high-tech night-vision cameras on the grounds. These would be linked up to my laptop so that, when I got home, I could monitor the footage and alert my clients to any significant activity (they only lived 200 yards away from the care home, so could hurry over if necessary). One camera would be trained on a strategically placed dish of dried fish, which I believed would be a surefire way to lure out a ravenous Columbus. I called it cat caviar because it was irresistible to felines, who could often smell its fishy odor for hundreds of yards.

With all this in mind, I popped back to the care

home to consult with the cat-loving nurse, who kindly gave us the green light to deploy our cameras. I happened to spot Gracie sitting in the TV room and I went over for a quick chat. Her eyes widened when she saw me approaching.

"Have you found the cat?"

"Not yet," I said, smiling, "but I have good reason to believe that he's been in your garden, maybe even pinching your cat food."

I then told her how Operation Columbus was going to work, explaining that, in addition to the cameras, I really needed an extra set of eyes to watch from indoors.

"D'you think that's something you could assist me with, Gracie?" I asked. "You'd be such a great help."

"You're asking me to help you?"

"Yes, I am. Consider yourself part of Team Molly tonight."

I was somewhat taken aback to see her eyes filling with tears. "How very kind of you to ask," she said, patting my hand. "It's nice to feel wanted, for a change. I'm afraid you tend to feel a bit invisible when you get past ninety."

What a delightful lady, I thought as I headed out of the care home and back to the car.

At about 9:45 that evening, a tired and hungry marmalade cat crept through the hole in the fence, padded over to the plate of fish and began to gobble up the morsels. At the same time, an elderly lady, sitting by her bedroom window, squinted through her black-rimmed spectacles at the shadowy four-legged figure. She let out a little coo of delight and swiftly telephoned the number on the Post-it note she'd been clasping since dinner.

Within two minutes, Columbus was back in the arms of his owner, and our happy ending was complete.

The following day, Molly and I returned to South London. Our first port of call was Kenneth's house, where,

Columbus at home after his ordeal

beside a huge, twinkling Christmas tree, we found Harriet and Columbus curled up together on the sofa.

Then it was time for a pit stop at the care home to pick up my assorted field cameras. Molly and I were ushered through the garden gate by the friendly nurse.

"I'm so glad I've seen you today, Mr. Butcher, because I wanted to thank you personally for being so kind to Gracie," she said. "She's a very bright lady, and I think she sometimes gets a little bored in here. But she was so happy at the breakfast table this morning. She couldn't stop smiling. She had to tell all the residents that she'd helped to solve Operation Columbus."

"Ah, that's lovely to hear." I smiled. "In fact, could you ensure she gets this?"

I fished a photo of Molly from my wallet and whipped out a pen from my pocket.

To Gracie, I wrote. *We couldn't have done it without you. Best wishes, Team Molly.*

By the time I'd packed all my cameras away, dusk had begun to set in. Instead of battling rush-hour traffic, I decided to make the five-minute drive to my favorite South London park. When we arrived, we walked a little farther afield, passing through a rather dense, muddy wooded area. We finally arrived at a clearing, where we spent a good forty minutes playing tug-of-war with a pair of knotted socks. Every now and then I'd let Molly win our tussle, and she'd run a few victory laps around me, the socks clenched between her teeth like a trophy. She would then bound back to my side for another round.

Eventually we wandered back to a food stand, where I ordered myself a hot chocolate and a bratwurst, as well as some water for Molly to accompany her treats. For a few minutes I sat on a nearby bench, watching the Ferris wheel slowly turning in the darkening sky, listening to the cheery chatter between families and friends. As Molly snuggled in closer, I could feel her heartbeat next to mine—*thumpity-thump, thumpity-thump*—and, as I so often did when we were together like this, I began chatting to her.

"Do you realize, Molly," I said, tenderly stroking her head, "that we've been together for nearly one whole year?"

She looked up at me and blinked those long eyelashes of hers, as if to say, *Really? Wow!*

"What an adventure we've had, eh?" I smiled. "All those lovely people we've met, and all those fabulous places we've visited."

I began to scroll through my memory bank, reeling off the names of some of the pets and clients whose lives had been touched by my amazing rescue dog. Tim and Rusty. Renu and Buffy. And, of course, Harriet and Columbus. Then I ran through a cast list of people who'd supported us along this wonderful journey: Claire, Rob,

Astrid and Mark at Medical Detection Dogs; my lovely friend Anna; my parents, my son, my girlfriend . . .

Quite suddenly, I noticed something white and fluffy landing on Molly's snout. And another. And then another. Molly shook herself awake and deftly sprang off my lap, and—much to the amusement of passersby—began to snap at the snowflakes that had started to spiral down from the sky.

Now this is what I call FUN, Dad! she seemed to say. *I haven't played in this white stuff for AGES!*

Here I was, in my favorite city, on a magical evening, spending quality time with my beautiful cocker spaniel.

You need to capture this moment, Colin, I said to myself.

So I angled my phone, held my dog close, flashed a big grin and took a quick selfie. The resulting photo made me smile and I promptly forwarded it to Sarah, along with a caption.

Molly and Me, it said.

EPILOGUE

Molly endured training in all conditions, even through the winter

My story began on the edges of the rainforests of Malaysia and Singapore, where my brother and I, accompanied by our faithful canine friends, scampered around like characters from a Rudyard Kipling novel. They were good years, full of incredible experiences, and most certainly influenced all my decisions on the pets I have owned.

In mid-December 2018 Molly passed the milestone of taking part in one hundred searches. She has now helped in the recovery of seventy-four missing cats, six dogs—and one Hermann's tortoise—many of which would have perished without her assistance. The other twenty-six cats have still not been found, although we did our utmost to locate them.

Molly is a truly remarkable dog and she never ceases to amaze me, constantly testing every rule I put in place, never fully accepting my right to impose my will upon her; though, why should she? We are, after all, a team and she deserves to be treated equally. She is an excellent problem-solver and remembers every location where she has found a missing cat. Her quickest recovery has been under five minutes.

Although Molly is prepared to share all that she knows about her world, the same cannot be said of cats. They have a reputation for being secretive and indifferent, often behaving in the most unpredictable way, happy one day and gone the next. However, I am an experienced detective and have learned the value of being patient. With every passing investigation, I discover just a little bit more about these supposedly furtive creatures and I am starting to identify patterns in their behavior, which is helping me to develop my understanding of why they go missing and, most importantly, where to start searching when they do. It seems to me that cats are not that secretive after all. An unhappy cat will often go to considerable lengths to let their owner know about their displeasure long before abandoning the family home. If you notice your cat behaving in an unusual way, then it's because your cat wants you to, so pay attention, because you could save yourself an awful lot of heartache.

On a final note, I would have loved to have included every case that we have investigated and to mention all the wonderful people that we have worked with, but there are simply too many for one book. In addition, there will be many more cases to investigate, and I also have plans to find a new apprentice . . . but that is a whole new story.

ACKNOWLEDGMENTS

I have dedicated my book to my brother David, who died just short of his twenty-first birthday, in the arms of his young wife, Katrina. In all the years that he struggled so ardently to defeat that awful disease, I never once heard him complain, he just soaked up everything life threw at him and soldiered on, always hoping that the doctors would make him better. To this day, I feel that my brother is watching over me, inspiring me to do the very best I can. He never gave up, so neither will I, and it's only with his guidance that I have managed to complete my journey with Molly. We proved the doubters wrong, David, and achieved what so many said could not be done. I only wish you were around to see it.

To my parents, I want to say thank you for allowing me the freedom to explore the natural world of Malaysia, Singapore and England, for the many animals you brought into my life and for press-ganging me into the Royal Navy. By the way, I'm sorry about the mice.

I know you always thought it was the cats that were bringing them home.

My journey from police officer to private sleuth and, finally, pet detective has been an incredibly rewarding experience and throughout my book I have given recognition to those who inspired or supported me along the way. There are, however, a few who I think are worthy of additional praise.

Both Sam and Stefan have left the company to follow different paths, but they remain good friends and always will be.

The three of us had some amazing adventures together, both as private sleuths and as pet detectives, and I could not have built UKPD without their loyalty and support. I am forever indebted to them.

Thank you to my good friend and canine guru Anna Webb. But for her, I would never have met the amazing team at Medical Detection Dogs. To Dr. Claire Guest, Dr. Astrid Concha, Rob Harris and Mark Doggett, to all the volunteers and Molly's foster family. You did a great job. Molly is a star.

To my agents, Rowan Lawton and Eugenie Furniss, thank you for putting your trust in me and for allowing me to tell my story my way, and to the Furniss and Lawton team, Rory, Rachel, Liane and Lucy, thank you for all your hard work in bringing my book to a global audience. My heartfelt thanks go to Joanne Lake, who has brought so much depth and color to my story and whose patience, expert advice and skill has helped to create such a wonderful tale. Thank you, Zennor Compton, whose enthusiasm and energy ensured I selected the right publisher, and to my editor, Charlotte Hardman, for her insight and professionalism and her ability to enhance the story.

To my darling Sarah, who has been so incredibly supportive and understanding over the last few years, for her intuition and wise counsel and, most of all, for accepting my troublesome and mischievous spaniel into her life.

Then there is my amazing, enchanting and adorable sidekick Molly. Without her, none of this would have been possible. She tests me relentlessly, always surprises me and never lets me down. She really is one in a million.

Finally, to all the pet owners who have put their faith and trust in Molly and me. Thank you for allowing us into your lives. We enjoyed meeting every single one of you.

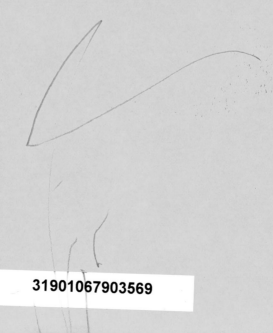